LOVE IN HINDU LITERATURE

LOVE
IN
HINDU LITERATURE

BENOY KUMAR SARKAR

GYAN

Published by

Gyan Publishing House
5, Ansari Road
Daryaganj, New Delhi-110002
Phone: 011-47034999, 9811692060
E-mail: books@gyanbooks.com

Distribution Network
gyanbooks.com
India, USA, Canada, UK, Australia, France

ISBN: 978-81-212-8572-8 (PB)
First Published, 1916

2nd Impression 2023

Printed at: Gyan Press, Delhi.

LOVE IN HINDU LITERATURE
Author: Benoy Kumar Sarkar

LOVE

IN

HINDU LITERATURE

BENOY KUMAR SARKAR

Author of *Chinese Religion Through Hindu Eyes*, *The Folk-Element in Hindu Culture*, *The Positive Background of Hindu Sociology*, *The Science of History and the Hope of Mankind*, etc.,
and Translator of *Sukra-nīti*
(Hindu Economics and Politics).

1916

MARUZEN COMPANY, LTD

TOKYO, KYOTO, OSAKA, FUKUOKA, & SENDAI

CONTENTS

PREFACE

LOVE between man and woman has always been a theme of Hindu poetry. With Kālidāsa, the Shakespeare or Goethe of classical Sanskrit literature, (who flourished in the first half of the fifth century in the reign of Chandragupta II, one of the Indian Charlemagnes), love between the sexes was a principal motif of his epic, lyric and dramatic works. But when a Hindu speaks of his love-literature, he thinks first and foremost of the mediaeval pastoral lyrics, the *Padābalī*, which may be conveniently described as the "Idylls of Rādhā," of which Rādhā is the heroine and Krishna or Kānu her lover. The present essay seeks mainly to interpret a few of these lyrics as englished by Dr. A. K. Coomāraswāmy.

In mediaeval Bengal writers on love were legion. They are commonly known as the trouveres or minstrels of Vaishnavism, a cult of *bhakti* or devotion, which corresponds to the Jōdō Buddhism of Japan and the Sufi mysticism of Persia. In Vaishnava parlance the name, Krishna, is divine, and Rādhā semi-divine. Rādhā-Krishna literature is thus liable to be regarded as an allegory of the mystical union between God and the Soul. The present writer pleads for a thoroughly human and secular interpretation, unless, of course, the relation between the sexes be considered as something spiritual or divine. The treatment of love by Vaishnava poets, by Vidyāpati in particular, is so plainly and emphatically in the language of the senses, that it is impossible to read any super-sensual meaning into it. If sexual love is mysticism, Vidyāpati is a mystic.

It has been a tendency among scholars, both Indian and foreign, writing on Hindu history, philosophy, science, literature, arts and crafts, and even industry, to label the successive stages in the evolution of Hindu culture with the exclusive hall-mark of one or other of the metaphysico-religious systems, e.g., Vedic, Upanishadic, Shaiva, Buddhist, Tāntric, Vaishnava, Jaina, Shākta, etc. India is generally presented to the world in terms of creeds, dogmas and rituals. The absurdity would be evident if one were to treat the whole course of Western civilization as nothing but Graeco-Roman paganism, Oriental Christianity, Lutheranism, Pilgrim Fathers, Oxford Movement, Unitarianism Christian Science, and so forth, in succession. Students of world-culture who are obsessed by the influence of religious ideas on human achievements would read in the *Aeneid* only a *purāna* of Latin mythology, in the *Divine Comedy* only an encyclopaedia of mediaeval Christianity, and in the *Paradise Lost* only a bible of the Puritans; or, where in modern literature and art, they find treatment of subjects from Hellenic mythology, they would be inclined to interpret it as "Back to paganism"! And they would surely evaluate the writings of Descartes, Hume, Kant, Tolstoy, Nietzsche, Emerson and Bergson, according to the conventional theological jargon, "christian," "non-christian," "anti-christian"!

This is exactly what has been done with regard to Hindu culture-history. The archaeologist, Vincent Smith, whose researches have unearthed a host of forgotten Frederick the Greats, Napoleons, Machiavellis, statesmen, generals, and other men of action from the Indian past, makes the following remark in concluding his *Early History of India*: "The most important branch of Indian history is the history of her thought." But is not the history of every other country also in the same sense the history of thought? An unbiassed application of the "comparative method" would yield the result (1) that Indian history is as great a history of enterprises, adventures, exploits and undertakings of a practical worldly character as the history of other peoples, and (2) that the history of other peoples is as great a record of speculation, thought, metaphysics, mysticism etc., as that of the Hindus.

The standard *History of Bengali Language and Literature* by Dines Chandra Sen is likewise vitiated by the same fallacy, which, originating in the nineteenth century, continues even now to be the first postulate and stock-in-trade of every indologist. In the story of a thousand years' literary development Sen has managed to watch only the struggle for supremacy among the various orders of gods and socio-religious systems. The great national epic of the Romans would have no significance to a critic like Sen except what may be gathered from the ultimate triumph of Venus over Juno in the life-history of Aeneas!

The poet, Rabīndranāth Tāgore, also, in his lectures and essays, has harped on the soul's yearning for the Infinite, the "quest of the Holy Grail," as being the chief ingredient in the *Indo Damashii*, the spirit of Hindusthān. An absurd position consistent with the poet's unhistorical way of studying history and social problems, which would reduce the ancient and mediaeval people of India almost into non-political, non-economic, invertebrate, backboneless human beings. Generally speaking, his method consists in taking one or two fine phrases from the Hindu classics without reference to the time or place of their origin, and summing up in them the "spirit" of India or the trend of Indian history, whether of the tenth century B.C. or of the tenth century A.D., whether of the Himālayan valleys or of the Bengal plains or of the Deccan trap. This would be like generalizing two thousand years of European history into one or two verse-maxims of the Hebrew Old Testament or Elizabethan England into a line of Shakespeare.

And Coomāraswāmy, to whom Young India owes a great part of the present-day art-consciousness as a factor in the nationalist movements, has also yielded to the same *idola* in the air when he discovers an excessive dose of *yoga* or *dhyāna*, i.e., meditation in Hindu sculptures and paintings. He seems to have lost his balance especially in his "elucidations" of the songs of Vidyāpati about the Rādhā-Krishna affair.

It is the object of the present essay to urge the need for a sober interpretation of the facts of Hindu life and movements. Even where the setting is religious or mythological and the *dramatis personae* divine or semi-divine, one need not be tempted to mean by them "more than what meets the ear." Ninetynine percent of what has been passing for other-worldly literature and art in India is really the literature and art of human passions, human ideals, human interests and conflicts. To be more definite, it may be said, that folk-life and sex-life have been the two chief motifs of a considerable portion of Indian thought. Most of the mediaeval writings, whether in Bengali, Hindi, Mārāthi, or Sanskrit, e.g., *Kavi-kamkana Chandī*, the *Purānas*, etc., have to be approached exactly as one approaches the works of Virgil, Dante and Milton, with the methodology of art-criticism.

Finally, it is submitted, again, that Vidyāpati has sung of love as every man and every woman understand it—love as understood by physiologists and psychologists—love as the subject-matter of *Kāma-shāstra* or erotics—love as the theme of Wagner's music-drama, *Tristan und Isolde*.

BENOY KUMAR SARKAR

Shanghai, China
April 15, 1916.

LOVE IN HINDU LITERATURE

India has been opened up from an interesting angle in Coomāraswāmy's *Songs of Vidyāpati*. After the appetite of the reading public, so far as things Indian may be said to have any reading public, has been jaded with too much of Tāgore's "offerings," ecstasies, Kabīrisms, and "dark chambers," the veteran student of Hindu art and art-history has come forward with a bit of India in its joy-form. He reveals to us a world in which the sweets of life turn even pangs into joys:

"Drunken are the honey-bees in honey-season
With the honey of the honey-flowers:
In Honey-Brindāban resides
The Honey-Lord of honey-love.
Amid the companies of honey-maids
Is honey-honey-dalliance:
Honeyed are the blissful instruments of music.
Honeyed hands are beating honey-measures.
Honeyed is the dance's sway,
Honeyed are the movements of the dancers,
Honeyed are their happy songs,
And honeyed are the words of Vidyāpati."

Vidyāpati is "roses, roses all the way," and is a veritable Spenserian "Bower of Bliss." His *Padābali*, or "The Idylls of Rādhā," are songs of Love and of lovers' ways, of Madana, the Lord of love, and of Vasanta or Spring, his friend, of chātakas and chakoras,[1]

---

1) partridge.

chakravākas[1] and mayuras,[2] of ashokas[3] and kadambas,[4] champakas[5] and tamālas,[6] of the dark Yamunā[7] and darker tresses of damsels, of the lovely moon and the lovelier "moon-face," of the clinking of the anklets and the flutter of the wimple, of the grove-trysts after night-fall and the "primrose path of dalliance," and of the thousand and one love-tonics furnished by nature or devised by art. Here we have "*The Earthly Paradise*," as it were, of an Indian William Morris.

I. TĀGORE.

It need be noted, however, at the very outset, that Coomāraswāmy's exhibiting of the India of joy and beauty is not the first in point of time. The Madana of Tāgore's *Chitrā* has already imported for us the "fragrant wine of heaven" from the "Divine storehouse," and we have watched how Arjuna "drains his first draught of pleasure," and Chitrā experiences the "rarest completion of life's desire, the first union of love." For this tiny lyrical play or dramatic lyric is indeed the most human and eminently readable of all Tāgore's efforts in English. The real "lyric of love and life" is not the *Gardener*, but *Chitrā*. Sonorous words, well-poised phrases, exquisite lines, and an almost perfect rhythm grace every page of this 'play' in one act, which is really a single sentiment done into a full-throated song long-drawn-out. And the very atmosphere of this delicate composition seems alive with intense passion.

1) *Anas casarca*, 2) peacock, 3) *Jonesia asoka*, 4) *Anthocephalus cadamba*, 5) *Michelia champaka*, 6) *Garcinia zanthochymus*, 7) river of that name.

It is the Petrarchan Italianated atmosphere of *Romeo and Juliet.*

Chitrā is a study in the sense-man, in the glories and enjoyments of the life in the flesh. "The southern breeze caressed me to sleep. From the flowering Mālatī bower overhead silent kisses dropped over my body. On my hair, my breast, my feet, each flower chose a bed to die on. I slept. And, suddenly in the depth of my sleep, I felt as if some intense eager look, like tapering fingers of flame, touched my slumbering body. I started up and saw the Hermit standing before me. The moon had moved to the west...... The air was heavy with perfume; the silence of the night was vocal with the chirping of cricket...... It seemed to me that I had, on opening my eyes, died to all realities of life and undergone a dream-birth into a shadow land. Shame slipped to my feet like loosened clothes. I heard his call—'Beloved, my most beloved!' And all my forgotten lives united as one and responded to it. I said, 'Take me, take all I am!' And I stretched out my arms to him. The moon set behind the trees. One curtain of darkness covered all...... With the first gleam of light...... I rose up...... He lay asleep with a vague smile about his lips." The whole scene reminds one of the "chamber of dreams" superintended by "the Spirit of Love" in Rossetti's *Dante's Dream.*

Further, "With green leaves wet from the spray of the foaming waterfall, I have made our noonday bed in cavern dark as night. There the cool of the soft green mosses thick on the black and dripping stone kisses your eyes to sleep. Let me guide you thither."

With all these we are refreshing our memory of

the mediaeval sonneteers of Europe and can be appreciative companions of the nearer Burns and Scott, Rossetti and Whitman. Sense-life with all its heat, the desire to "see perfect completeness once and forever," the mad festivals of this earth, for which men and women would gladly forego the doubtful happiness of life in paradise, "a breast whose blood's a troubled ocean, each throb the earthquake's wild commotion," "a crystal brow, the moon's despair," and "lips that seem on roses fed," these are the stuff out of which Tāgore has shapen this delightful little work.

Prof. Jadunāth Sarkār has said: "*Chitrā* is no mere tale of joys and of a lover and his lass. It is a criticism of life." As if a tale of "a lover and his lass" is not a criticism of life! Further, it may be asked: "Which piece of world's art has not been a criticism of life? i.e., has not brought with it its own system of life's values?" Every artist has been necessarily a critic of life, a moralizer, even inspite of himself sometimes, and has attempted, consciously or unconsciously, an answer to the greatest of all questions, the question, "How to live?" Didactic Poetry is indeed a tautology if not "a contradiction in terms;" as psychologically it is impossible to conceive an "art for art's sake." Every art-work is bound to be a criticism of life. The chief question always is "What criticism? What transvaluation of values? What suggestions for a new life?"

With regard to *Chitrā* Mr. Sarkār would have us believe that "the moral never overshadows the story, but...... that he who runs may read it." Let us read it. In the last scene Chitrā throws off the disguise and tells her sweetheart, the hero Arjuna, that she is nourishing his babe in her womb. Like Goethe, whose son had been born eighteen years before he married his mistress, Arjuna is thus the father of a bastard, and Chitrā a silly indiscreet maiden! Probably even the extreme wing of Ibsenists and Mormonists would not appreciate "illegitimacy." And yet it is apparent that the whole story leads but to this.

There are fine sentiments about the graces and advantages of home-life, the womanhood of woman, and the glorification of service and duty. If such passages were to be gleaned and placed together in order to indicate the moral or philosophy of the poem, the statements of Iago, Iachimo and Regan could be palmed down as the philosophy of Shakespearean art! Rather, it must be remarked that these statements about home and its sanctity do not form an integral part of the plot in this little play. Besides, they come in after the heroine has been *enceinte*. What, then, is the "criticism of life" in *Chitrā*?

To do justice to the poet we must look upon Chitrā not as the "Princess" of Tennyson, but as the "Highland girl" of Wordsworth. Tāgore has presented us with a Chitrā about whom, like the adventurer Arjuna, we may remark in the words of the English romanticist:

"In truth together ye do seem
Like something fashion'd in a dream.

* * *

Thou wear'st upon thy forehead clear
The freedom of a mountaineer.

* * *

Thou art to me but as a wave
Of the wild sea.

* * *

The lake, the bay, the waterfall;
And Thee, the spirit of them all!"

The questions that naturally arise about Tāgore's Chitrā as she appears to the puissant-armed hero must be like the following:

"Who was her father?
Who was her mother?
Had she a sister?
Had she a brother?"

And, in fact, Tāgore puts almost the same questions in Arjuna's mouth: "My love, have you no home where kind hearts are waiting for your return? A home which you once made sweet with your gentle service and whose light went out when you left it out for this wilderness?" It should be noted, in passing, that this picture of a sweet home is only an incidental inquiry on the part of the lover to satisfy a curiosity or solve his mystery regarding the person with whom he has been enjoying all this while, and has not even an indirect reference to the prospective abode of Arjuna and his unmarried darling.

Chitrā has always been to our hero "a wave of the wild sea," a mystery; and Tāgore does not want to solve this mystery. For the heroine is made to keep up the mystery: "Why these questions?...... Do you not know that I am no more than what you see before you? For me there is no vista beyond." And to the more definite desire of Arjuna to let his heart feel Chitrā on all sides and live with her in the peaceful security of love, she presents but another mystifying remark: "Why this vain effort to catch and keep the tints of the clouds, the dance of the waves, the smell of the flowers?"

Certainly Chitrā is not to Arjuna a Tennyson's princess, but a Wordsworthian "solitary reaper," or, as we have quoted above, a "wave of the sea." Chitrā is what Shelley would have liked most, a "clanless," tribeless, society-less girl, without a "vista beyond," without the "bonds of name and home and parentage." She eludes everybody's group. It is the community of communityless Chitrās which Shelley wanted to evolve out of the debris of the present-day convention-ridden world. Chitrā is "absolute," "unconditioned," "free," a part of the elemental forces, the "spirit of them all," —the exact antipodes of Tennyson's princess who is bound to be the keystone of a social arch.

And the plot is laid in a scene which is the farthest removed from the family, the society and the state. "See how the rain pours in torrents and fiercely beats upon the hillside. The dark shadow of the clouds hangs heavily over the forest, and the swollen stream, like reckless youth, overleaps all barriers with mocking laughter." It is a place where robbers often pour from the northern hills like a mountain flood to devastate the village. Hither our renowned hero, the world-conquering Arjuna, has retired to observe his vow of celibacy for twelve years. The first human being he meets here is a hunter, and the next the rustics afraid of robbers.

The writer has told the original story as given in the *Mahābhārata*, in his preface. But we have not been instructed to understand the play in the light of the preface. Nor is it necessary to do so. We are to take the composition as it is without reference to the preface, without the context of the Hindu tradition in literature or life. And the reader is presented with the following episodes. Chitrā finds out the identity of the hermit-hero, "the one great idol of her dreams." "Then by the boon of gods I obtained for a year the most radiant form that a mortal ever wore." And the very first overture on the great warrior tells its tale. He is compelled to accept "his rebellion's sentence" at her hand. His vow of chastity crumbles away at the first touch of beauty. The lovesick hero confesses to Chitrā's "superbly beautiful" disguise: "Ah, I feel how vain is fame, the pride of prowess! Everything seems to me a dream. You alone are perfect; you are the wealth of the world, the end of all poverty, the goal of all efforts, the one woman!" Mars submits to Cupid. The vow of the sternest and austerest of all Kshatriyas has been dissolved "even as the moon dissolves the night's vow of obscurity." The triumph of Love is complete. Arjuna henceforth lives, as it were, in a dream, a life of trance; and till the close of the story he has to admit the spell of Chitrā on his life: "You seem to me like a goddess hidden within a golden image. I cannot touch you, I cannot pay you my dues in return for your priceless gifts." This is the "mystery" of love, and what are those priceless gifts? Chitrā explains the great "riddle of the universe:" "The gift that I proudly bring you is the heart of a woman." And certainly the proudest and mightiest of heroes is too poor to offer anything in return for that.

All through the poem we find our brave world-conqueror amazed and almost confounded in the "magic circle" of love.

Lili's spell over Goethe is thus described:

"Heart, my heart, what is this feeling,
That doth weigh on thee so sore?
What new life art thou revealing
That I know myself no more?
Gone is all that once was dearest,
Gone the care that once was nearest,
Gone the labour, gone the bliss,
Ah! whence comes such change as this?

* * *

With such magic-web she binds me,
To burst through I have no skill;
All-absorbing passion blinds me,
Paralyses my poor will.
In her charméd sphere delaying,
I must live, her will obeying."

If the exquisite little story has any 'criticism of life,' it is a very simple one. It is an extollation, an apotheosis, of the "heart of a woman." It is the influence of Beatrice upon Dante. The author has not preached here any ism, he has no philosophy of social reconstruction to offer; he is neither a Nietzschean nor a Blakist, neither a Shavian nor an Ibsenist; he is not an advocate of "free love" or clandestine connexions; he is not preaching the sanctity of home or the duties of married life; he is neither pro-nor anti-suffragist; he is not a feminist, not a misogynist; his sole aim is to delineate with just a few simple touches one of the elemental passions, feelings, affections or sentiments of human life. His attitude is a thoroughly non-moral one. He has thrown a man and a woman together, and the result is what you see. You need know nothing more about Arjuna and Chitrā than what has been given in the play, and you see that love, that most mysterious and romantic of all terms in human vocabulary, is at bottom the name for sex-instinct, sex-impulse, sex-affection or sex-relation,—a helpless and hopeless submission to "the most radiant form that a mortal ever wore"—the homage to Beauty.

The artist has concentrated his whole attention only on one aspect of human life—the relation between man and woman. And with regard to this also he has eliminated as many considerations as possible. He has tried to give us a working "hypothesis" of the mystery of the female heart, or the secret of the attraction which has its final consummation in marriage, family, society, church, and state.

In physical and social siences we are familiar with the method of conducting experiments by elimination, inhibition, etc. We are asked to conceive things which do not actually exist, e.g., length without breadth, motion without friction, force without matter, the terrestrial system without gravitation, the "ideal gas" of Guy-Lussac, the "absolute" solid, conditions of "absolute" equilibrium, "stationary" state, the "representative firm," the "normal" prices, and so forth. The object in each case is not to regard the problems of nature and society as really simple, but only to 'specialize' in each aspect of the problem and try to understand separately in their elemental condition all the strands that constitute the complex web. The result is a "working hypothesis" in each instance; and it postulates the possibility of modification through the introduction of new conditions.

Tāgore's *Chitrā* is a study of love "in vacuum," if I may use this expression from physics. It is a study in "absolute" love, love detached, for the time being, from all "bonds of name and home and parentage," love unhampered by considerations of economic necessity, race-conservation, political power, and military efficiency. Not that these considerations are worth nothing, but those considerations are inhibited in *Chitrā*. Incidentally one or other of these considerations may have been taken in, but the primary motif of the lyric is the profoundest physiological truth that sex-attraction is at once the origin and fundamental nature of love.

It is for this reason that Arjuna knows nothing about Chitrā, and Chitrā purposely mystifies her lover. Chitrā seems to say: "You know me, Arjuna; and I know you. The profane and philistine world need not pry into our sacred relation." As for Arjuna, he feels the spell of the female heart long before he is aroused from reverie to ask a Keats-like question: "Was it a vision or a waking dream?...... Do I wake or sleep?" And when Chitrā speaks to him about his babe in her womb, he accepts that solid fact as a matter of course. It is the consummation of the mysterious relation which he has never understood. Tāgore's Arjuna is *mere* man, and Chitrā *mere* woman. In a sequel to *Chitrā*, the babe, "a second Arjuna," may turn out to be a Hindu Perseus the Deliverer; but the theme of the present work is complete without that. Mortal Arjuna has already known "love's satiety,": as he confesses, "Beloved, my life is full."

Chitrā is thus an artist's study in sex. It touches the very foundations of individual life, and thus of social existence as well. The sex-element in human relations is at once their imperfection and their grandeur. *Chitrā* announces in unmistakable terms the sacredness of this sex-impulse, the sanctity of this sex-attraction. We know what Wordsworth said, from his own experience, for all mankind, regarding the successive manifestations of the sex-idea on man's side in his relation with woman :

"She was a phantom of delight
When first she gleam'd upon my sight ;
A lovely apparition sent

* * *

To haunt, to startle and waylay."

Chitrā did really "haunt, startle and waylay" our man with a mission.

In the next stage, Wordsworth's woman is

"A creature not too bright or good
For human nature's daily food,
For transient sorrows, simple wiles,
Praise, blame, love, kisses, tears and smiles."

The following is the lecture of Chitrā to her spell-bound lover: "I am Chitrā. No goddess to be worshipped, nor yet the object of common pity to be brushed aside like a moth with indifference." Further, "I am not beautifully perfect...... I have many flaws and blemishes ...... My garments are dirty, and my feet are bleeding with thorns...... The gift that I proudly bring you is the heart of a woman. Here have all pains and joys gathered, the hopes and fears and shames of a daughter of the dust; here love springs up struggling toward immortal life." Thus the dirt, the dust, the flesh, the sense, constitute the very essence of the female heart; and these are not to be ignored though the "immortal" is also to be striven for.

Lastly, "with eye serene," Wordsworth sees

"A perfect woman nobly plann'd
To warn, to comfort, and command;
And yet a spirit still, and bright
With something of an angel-light."

This is our Chitrā's love springing "up struggling toward immortal life." Adds the Hindu damsel: "Herein lies an imperfection which yet is noble and grand."

Rabīndranāth Tāgore has then come out in his *Chitrā* with a study of "absolute" love or sex-impulse, the message of the sacredness of sex-attraction and the apotheosis of the "heart of a woman," wherein "lies an imperfection which yet is noble and grand." *Chitrā* is a bold contribution and is destined to live longer than *Gītānjali*.

II. KĀLIDĀSA.

Chitrā is a picture of love in its "naked dignity," divested of all ornaments, of love as "the-thing-in-itself," of love unconditioned by the Kantian categories of Time and Space. And *Chitrā* is not unique in Indian literature. The whole mass of mediaeval Rādhā-Krishna literature is based on this conception of love "in vacuum," of "absolute" love, of love as the "thing in itself," of love unhampered by considerations of economic struggle, domestic restraints, political might and military efficiency, i.e., of love as a function of sex and as a homage to beauty. The still earlier *Shakuntalā* and *Vikramorvasie* of the immortal Kālidāsa are probably the first literary works dealing more or less with love in its naked dignity, announcing the dignity of sex independent of all extraneous paraphernalia. Chitrā is *mere* woman, Rādhā is *mere* woman, Shakuntalā is *mere* woman to a considerable extent, Urvasie is *mere* woman to a considerable extent. These *mere* women are, so to speak, the feminine "sexual types" of present-day science, or the female "ideas" of Platonic philosophy.

All these girls are the nymphs of Arcadias. They are neither town-bred maidens nor country-women. They are the denizens of forests, hills and murmuring brooks. About each of them Dame Nature may be believed to have said:

"She shall be sportive as the fawn
That wild with glee across the lawn
Or up the mountain springs.
Nor shall she fail to see
E'en in motions of the storm
Grace that shall mould the maiden's form
By silent sympathy.
And vital feelings of delight
Shall rear her form to stately height,
Her virgin bosom swell."

All these maidens are lovers at first sight. Their life and surroundings are altogether such stuff as pastorals are made on. They are not suitable characters for

Tennyson's *Princess* or even the *Idylls of the King*. They are all "Highland girls," fit companions, if at all, of the "Sicilian Muse's" Corydon and Thyrsis, Phillis and Thestylis..

The moral or rather un-moral environment of the Chitrās, Rādhās and Urvasies of Hindu art can be understood from the following words of Goethe:

> "In the heroical age, when goddess and god were the lovers,
> Scarce did they look, but they long'd, longing they rush'd to enjoy.
> Think'st thou Love's goddess hung back, when deep in the forest of Ida,
> She, with a thrill of delight, first her Anchises beheld?
> Coyly had Luna delayed to fondle the beautiful sleeper,
> Soon had Aurora in spite waken'd the boy from his dream."

The most enchanting of Hindu pastoral idylls are the Rādhā-songs, the most romantic of Indian arcadias is Brindāban, and the most representative Hindu Theocritus is Vidyāpati.

I have mentioned the lyrical love-dramas of Kālidāsa in the same breath with Tāgore and Vidyāpati. It is questionable, however, if the Kālidāsan treatment of love is exactly of a piece with the mediaeval and modern Hindu treatment. His heroines of the two plays are *mere* women and yet something more. His pictures of love "in vacuum" are greatly coloured by extraneous considerations. The "criticism of life" furnished by him is thus less "hypothetical" and more complete than that in *Chitrā*; because he has cared to introduce fuller details into the "magic circle" of love.

To take *Vikramorvasie*, englished as the *Hero and the Nymph* by Aurobinda Ghosh. It was suggested that the sequel to Tāgore's *Chitrā* might give us a Perseus the Deliverer in "the second Arjuna" for all that we know. It is exactly this sequel which has been developed by Kālidāsa and made an integral part of the events commencing with love at first sight. We need not scrutinize too minutely the technique and dramatic machinery as well as the supernatural elements in Kālidāsa's work, nor discuss the justice of the treatment meted out to the first wife of the hero. But we notice that Urvasie has become the queen of King Pururavas. We learn—

> "All thy allotted days
> This Urvasie is given thee for wife
> And lovely helpmeet."

We are told likewise that the crown-prince has been taught "letters, scripture, arts,—

> Last, every war-like science;"

and Pururavas is "grown a glorious father in this boy."

We are allowed to see the scene where at the very sight of her child, Urvasie's "veiled bosom" heaves towards him and gets "wet with milk." And we hear the son's sentiments in the following words:

> "O how must children on their father's knees
> Grown great be melted with a filial sweetness,
> When only hearing that this is my father
> I feel I love him."

Nor are these domestic scenes alone the new conditions to which readers see the love at first sight harnessed. Serious considerations of state and war also have been introduced to make the picture as true to life as possible. Thus Pururavas is confident about the fitness of his young son to take charge of his empire because he is a "ruler born":

"The ichorous elephant
Not yet full-grown tames all the trumpetings
Of older rivals......
So is it with the ruler born:
His boyish hand inarms the sceptered world.
The force that rises with its task, springs not
From years, but is a self-and in-born greatness."

Of the not distant call to arms and "mobilization" also we get news:

"These divulge
Advent of battle and the near uprise
Of Titans warring against Gods. Heaven needs
Thee, her great soldier;"

and the last incident in the drama leaves us with the idea of an alliance between Heaven and Earth against the Titans and a virtual declaration of war:

"Thy son's great coronation mindeth me
Of yet another proud investiture,—
Kārtikeya crowned by Maghavān, to lead
Heaven's armies."

Thus the son of Vikrama and Urvasie will be a "Perseus the Deliverer" conceived by the Bengali philosopher-poet Aurobinda Ghosh, or an Andreas Hofer, the anti-Napoleonist hero of the hill-peasants of Tirol. He is to be the comrade-in-arms of the War-Lord of Heaven;

and the hero and the nymph will "unsundered live in sweetness conjugal."

But all this grows out of the whole Arjuna-Chitrā affair. The stoutest Bushidō-trained warriors cannot withstand the arrow from Cupid's bow. Love-smitten Vikrama is as helpless and miserable as the idol of our Chitrā's dream:

"No sooner seen than in my heart she leaped.
O easy entrance! since the bannered love
With his unerring shaft had made the breach
Where she came burning in."

Again, "Neither smoothest flowers,
Moonlight nor sandal visiting every limb
Nor necklaces of cool delight pearl,
Only heaven's nymph can perfectly expel
With bliss, or else—......
Speech secret full of her unedge my pangs."

The ecstasy of union over which Chitrā almost fainted is thus described by Kālidāsa:

"How does the winning of one loved augment
Sweet contradictions! These are the very rays
Of moonlight burned me late, and now they soothe;
Love's wounding shafts caress the heart like flowers,
Thou being with me; all natural sights and sounds
Once rude and hurtful, now caressing come
Softly, because of thee in my embrace."

And what is that woman whom Vikrama loves at first sight?

"In the process beautiful
Of her creation Heaven's enchanting moon
Took the creator's place, or very Love
Grown all amorousness, or else the mouth

Of honey and its days deep-mined with bloom."

So much for her creation. As for her beauty, Kālidāsa's hero speaks:

"Who could with words describe each perfect limb
Of that celestial whole? Take her in brief,
O friend, for she is ornament's ornament,
And jewels cannot make her beautiful.
They from her body get their grace. And when
You search the universe for similes,
Her greater beauty drives you to express
Fair things by her, not her by lesser fairness:
So she's perfection's model."

Arjuna also declared to Chitrā: "You alone are perfect...... the one woman. Others there are who can be but slowly known. While to see you for a moment is to see perfect completeness once and forever."

In *Vikramorvasie* as in *Chitrā* we are never far from sense-life, the "dirt," "the dust," the pleasures and pains of animal life, the joys and beauties of this fair earth. We are perpetually feeling that love is sex-hunger in origin and nature. The following wish of Pururavas is the burden of both these studies in love:

"When I had not embraced Thee, my desire,
One night in passing seemed a hundred nights;
O now if darkness would extend my joys
To equal length of real hours with this
Sweet face upon my bosom, I were blest."

The dignity of sex, the sanctity of love at first sight, the conception of love as homage to beauty, are as prominent in Kālidāsa as in Tāgore. We see Urvasie as wife, queen, and mother; nevertheless, the Chitrā-element in Urvasie pervades the whole work, and Arjuna can easily change place with Vikrama.

III. VIDYĀPATI.

Tāgore has given through Chitrā's lips the almost Wordsworthian philosophy of the "heart of a woman"; but in his treatment of the subject we meet with only "the phantom of delight." In Kālidāsa's treatment we see not only this but also something more. In Vidyāpati, however, we have neither this something more nor the Wordsworthian lecture. His treatment of love is emphatically the treatment of love "in vacuum," of love unconditioned, of love as a function of sex. Chitrā without her lecture on love and womanhood is Rādhā. Rādhā is *mere* woman, as her darling Krishna is *mere* man. The apotheosis of the sex-element in human relations has not been carried to a greater height in Indian literature than in Vidyāpati. The keynote of his idylls, as of the work of no other Hindu poet, can be best given in the following line of Keats:

"A thing of beauty is a joy for ever."

Coomāraswāmy begins his work on Vidyāpati with the dictum of the Persian poet, Shamsi Tabriz: "Be drunken with love, for love is all that exists." Another motto has been selected from William Blake: "The whole creation will be consumed and appear infinite and holy, whereas it now appears finite and corrupt. This will come to pass by an improvement of sensual enjoyment."

Vidyāpati is the very well of sensual enjoyment, of beauty and joy, and of the sweets of this earth. The following is a picture of his "thing of beauty:"

"Gainlier than a royal olifant, more graceful than the swan,
She goes to keep her tryst:
Her glorious body far surpasses any golden bud,
Or flawless flash of lightning.
Her tresses far surpass the clouds, the night the yak,
Or bees or moss:
Her eye-brow-tendril set on a crescent brow, surpasses
Bow and bees and snakes.
Her face excels the golden mirror, the moon, the lily,
Her lips the bimba fruit and coral:
Her teeth surpass the pearl, the jasmine and the granate seed,
Her neck the figure of the conch.
Her beauteous breasts surpass the honey-apple, or cymbals twain,
Or golden jars, mountains, or goblets:
Her arms excel the lotus-root and jungle-rope,
Her waist the drum's and lion's,
Softer than moss her vine of down and darker than the surm,
The triple folds are lovelier than rolling waves:
Her navel far surpasses any lake, or louts-leaves,
Her buttocks, head of olifant.
Her thighs excel the plantain stem, or trunk of royal olifant,
Her hands and feet, the lotus of the land:
Her nails surpass pomegranate seeds, the moon, or gems,
Her speech is more than nectar-sweet.

Says Vidyāpati: her shape is unsurpassed,
Peerless is Rādhā's beauty."

Vidyāpati's Rādhā is all flesh. The whole description is an aphrodisiac, pure and simple. As to the manner or style of portraiture, he resembles the earlier Kālidāsa in his selection of images and conceits from homely experiences and the natural surroundings. But in Tāgore's treatment of beauty we are in a less homely atmosphere though we get a subjective analysis and an insight into the inner self. In European literature also we find the same difference in treatment between the mediaevals and the moderns. The realistic coarseness and objective studies in *Le Roman de la Rose* are well known.

The following is the description of a non-pareil by an Elizabethan:

"Like to the clear in highest sphere
Where all imperial glory shines,
Of selfsame colour is her hair
Whether unfolded or in twines:
Heigh ho, fair Rosaline!
Her eyes are sapphires set in snow

* * *

Her cheeks are like the blushing cloud
That beautifies Aurora's face,

* * *

Her lips are like two budded roses
Whom ranks of lilies neighbour nigh,
Within which bounds she balm encloses
Apt to entice a deity:
Heigh ho, would she were mine!
Her neck is like a stately tower
Where Love himself imprison'd lies,

To watch for glances every hour
From her divine and sacred eyes;

* * *

Her paps are centres of delight,
Her breasts are orbs of heavenly frame,
Where nature moulds the dew of light
To feed perfection with the same.

* * *

With orient pearl, with ruby red,
With marble white, with sapphire blue
Her body every way is fed,
Yet soft in touch and and sweet in view."

It is this carnal beauty which is "a joy for ever" to the mediaeval Hindu poet. The *Padābalī* are the songs of delight in the flesh.

Rādhā's raptures over the first sight of her beloved Kānu are thus described:

"I cannot tell what that dear thief has done to me,—
When I beheld him, he did steal my heart, and went away,—
And as he went he showed so many signs of love,
The more I would forget, the less I may!"

This emotion we find in Shakespeare's Juliet also. Love at first sight must manifest itself in the same way whether in "Desert Cathay" or chilly Labrador.

The sentiment in the last line is expressed in the following lines of a Japanese poet of the eleventh century:

"'T were best to think no more of thee,
And let thee go, but yet
I never can forget."

The English version is by Porter and is taken from "*A Hundred Verses of Old Japan.*

The following is Vidyāpati's picture of separation between the lover and his sweet-heart:

"Can I forget,......
How when I took her hands, and went my way
to Mathurā,
She fell and fainted?
Nor with what trembling speech and gentle
murmuring
The fair and gentle creature spake?
My body stiffened, I came away indeed,
But there was left my heart with her.
Now lacking her, the day and night are dimmed
She is established in my heart:
Beside another love in regal state,
I live like any anchorite!"

Here is the memory of the parting "in silence and tears." The same sentiment of devotion to the sweet little nest in a darling's heart is expressed by Burns in the following promise of constancy:

"As fair art thou, my bonnie lass,
So deep in luve am I:
And I will luve thee still, my dear,
Till a' the seas gang dry:
Till a' the seas gang dry, my dear,
And the rocks melt wi' the sun;
I will luve thee still, my dear,
While the sands o' life shall run.
And fare thee weel, my only Luve!
And fare thee weel a while!

And I will come again, my Luve,
Tho' it were ten thousand mile."

Constancy in love, as that of the mandarin duck and drake, is also the theme of the famous tragic poem in Chinese, "The *Everlasting Wrong*," by Po Chu-i of the ninth century. The following is from Giles' *History of Chinese Literature* :

"At midnight, when none were near,
he had whispered in her ear,
'I swear that we will fly
like the one-winged birds,
Or grow united like the tree
with branches which twine together'"

And the heroine, who had been put to death by soldiers, is represented as having sent, through a Tāoist priest, the following message to her Imperial lover, from the spirit-land :

"Tell him," she said, "to be firm of heart,
as this gold and enamel,
And then in heaven or on earth below
We two may meet once more."

The pangs of separation and the desire for eternal companionship are the commonplaces of love-relations. A Japanese poet of the twelfth century thus describes the hope of reunion between two lovers parted by force :

"The rock divides the stream in two,
And both with might and main
Go tumbling down the waterfall ;
But well I know the twain
Will soon unite again."

The same sentiment finds expression in *A Maiden's*

Reverie, a Chinese poem of the third century B.C., englished by Budd:

"And though the seas divide us
Our hearts are one for ay,
And in sweet dreams will mingle
Until the meeting day."

This Chinese maiden's longing for her lover can be aptly compared in many of its particulars with the varying phases of Rādhā's expectant mood when her Kānu is away:

"The plum-tree's flower awakens
Thoughts of my lover now,
And I would pluck some blossoms
And send to far Sichow.
A gentle breeze is blowing,
The night is bright as day;
I will go and gather lilies,
And meet him on the way.
I put some in my bosom,
For the core is red as blood,
As the heart of a true lover,
When love is at the flood.
Above my head in batches
The wild geese northward hie,
And they will pass o'er Si-chow
Oh, would that I could fly!
But though my heart is weary,
I trust my lover's vow;
The south wind knows my longings
And will bear them to Sichow."

The treatment of wind and clouds and birds as messengers of love, and the use of stars and the moon and rain and flowers as the awakener of memories, are as common today as in ancient and mediaeval times. The longing of a modern lover is given below:

"Night and the shadow falling
Over land and sea,
Somewhere a voice is calling,
Calling for me.
Night and the stars are gleaming
Tender and true;
Dearest, my heart is dreaming,
Dreaming of you."

The following is another Chinese poem on the thoughts of a "love-laden soul":

"I know the endless distance
Must shut you from my view,
But the flower's gentle fragrance
Brings sweetest thoughts of you.
And, though it is but a trifle,
Which none would prize for gain,
It oft renews our parting,
With all the love and pain."

Vidyāpati is probably more intense than any poet who has worked on the longings of love-lorn hearts:

"The flowers are blowing in every glade,
Now spring has come, my dear,
The host of koils spread their noise:
My darling is abroad, I may no more sustain!"

Again, "If the flower be scorched by the summer sun,
What shall avail the autumn rains?
If I waste in longing this fresh young life,
What shall avail my Lover's love?"

Further, "Shatter my bangles of shell, take off my fine array,

And break my necklace of ivory-pearls,—
If my dear will forsake me, what is the use of jewels?
Cast them all in the waves of the Jumnā."

Vidyāpati's sole delight is in the joys of "this fresh young life," the happy thought of a life of roses without thorns, the hope of never parting from one's beloved, the sleepless nights of the young bride, the perpetual round of worldly bliss. He is not satisfied with merely suggestive touches. The following lines of a Japanese poet of the tenth century, for example, would be too cold and mild for Vidyāpati:

"Alas! the blush upon my cheek,
Conceal it as I may,
Proclaims to all that I am in love,
Till people smile and say—
'Where are thy thoughts today?"

Even the ordinary mood of Vidyāpati is far more vehement:

"To hide my body on either side revealed the other,
(O open wide and let me sink into the earth!)
Seeking to cover my breasts with my hands, I could not"—

Or, "I was alone, and weaving garlands,
My skirt and bodice were unloose,
And then came Kānu with quiet smiles!
How shall I hide my bosom and my girdle stead?"

Rādhā is anticipating the pleasure of reunion with her darling:

"He will take my hands and set me down on his lap,
He will soothe my heart for endless time:

I shall clasp him close, casting out coldness,
He will fill me with balm, I shall close my eyes ! "

The actual reunion is thus described :

" Each on the other's countenance gazing, twain are rapt—
Each in the other's arms the other infolds—
Twain are the mouths contented each with the nectar of other's lips."

Also, " The twain beyond speech are out of all reason,
The loveling disports with most ardent passion :
Eagerly fair-face kisses love-face
The bending moon drinks up the lotus."

Thus from beginning to end Vidyāpati has sung of the glories of life in the flesh. Like Keats, he would like to be

" Pillow'd upon my fair Love's ripening breast
To feel for ever its soft fall and swell,
Awake for ever in a sweet unrest ;
Still, still to hear her tender-taken breath
And so live ever,—or else swoon to death."

Or, as Bryon has put it more boisterously in his *All for Love*," to Vidyāpati

" The days of our youth are the days of our glory ;
And the myrtle and ivy of sweet two and twenty
Are worth all your laurels though ever so plenty."

The burden of our " honey-worded " " honey-poet " is ever the following :

" O, for a draught of vintage, that hath been
Cool'd a long age in the deep-delved earth,
Tasting of Flora and the country-green,
Dance, and provencal song, and sun-burnt mirth."

Vidyāpati would have none of, and would fain create a world without,

"The weariness, the fever, and the fret
Here, where men sit and hear each other groan;
Where palsy shakes a few, and, last gray hairs,
Where youth grows pale, and spectre-thin and dies;
Where but to think is to be full of sorrow
And leaden-eyed despairs;
Where Beauty cannot keep her lustrous eyes,
Or new Love pine at them beyond tomorrow."

His pastorals are alive in the perpetual spring of an Indian arcadia. He has given us legion of Tāgore's *Phālgunīs*. Shelley might have addressed the following to Vidyāpati's Rādhā or Krishna:

"With thy clear keen joyance
Langour cannot be:
Shadow of annoyance
Never came near thee:
Thou lovest; but never knew love's sad satiety."

Tāgore's Arjuna comes at length to a stage of "love's sad satiety." "Beloved, my life is full" was his last word to Chitrā. But the very Spirit of Love, the eternal fountain of sex-pleasure, seems to have been split into two, the male element (Purusha) and the female element (Prakriti), two sexual "types" or "ideas," in Vidyāpati's hero and heroine. This is Vidyāpati's "criticism of life." He is a phase of the Shelley of mediaeval India—the prophet of beauty in the flesh—the idealist of life in the sex—the "Spirit fierce," the "Thou, O uncontrollable," the "wild West Wind," of a fundamental human passion, of which the "imperfection" "yet is noble and grand."

In approaching this Hindu Theocritus under the guidance of Coomāraswāmy we have the rare advantage of perceiving the same universe through two distinct sense-organs. We enjoy this Indian atmosphere of beauty not only through our ears, but it has also been possible for us to actually visualize it. We hear the lovers' songs as well as see the world of love and lovers. Coomāraswāmy has illustrated his eleven chapters each with a painting of the later-mediaeval Rājput-Pāhāri school, e.g., of the seventeenth and eighteenth centuries. These are all collections from Kangra, Chamba and other Punjab hill-states far off from Mithilā in Eastern India, the land of Vidyāpati. The poet flourished in the fifteenth century, his earlier life being synchronous with the *Canterbury Tales* period of Chaucer.

There is thus the greatest discrepancy imaginable between Coomāraswāmy's singer-musician-poet and the painters both in time and space. But it is this discrepancy which all the more forces on us the conviction that all art is one, nay, that sense-organs are fundamentally one. We drink Nature through our eyes, we drink the world through our ears, just as we suck the soul through our lips. Every illustration of Coomāraswāmy is a verse in colours just as every verse is a picture in words, or every song a painting in sounds. The eleven pieces of painting are so many songs of sex-life, just as the *Padābalī* constitute a tapestry of love as "the-thing-in-itself." We have the Grecian Urn as well as the *Ode on the Grecian Urn* just in our front.

IV. ALLEGORY OF "THE HEART OF A WOMAN."

Coomāraswāmy, the poet and artist, as *unconscious* interpreter of Vidyāpati, has been a safe guide in our travels through "the realms of gold." But Coomāraswāmy the *conscious* interpreter, the art-critic and the annotator, does not seem to be so safe. I am not speaking of his works on art-history and art-criticism, e.g., those like *The Arts and Crafts of India and Ceylon*. I refer to the Notes (or "Elucidations" as he says) and Introduction to his illustrated edition of the *Padābalī*. He has not spoken out sufficiently "loud and bold." There is a latent dualism, I might almost say duplicity, an inconsistency, I might almost say insincerity, in his prose-explanations. And all this simply because he has fought shy of the only motif of this pastoral art which could never be missed.

In the first place, is the Rādhā-Krishna literature an allegory? Was Vidyāpati an allegorist? The answer must be an emphatic No. If Rādhā-Krishna literature is to be treated as allegorical, every bit of literary, plastic and other arts which has ever been the handiwork of man, must be regarded as allegory, i.e., as something "where more is meant than meets the ear." The Homeric *Iliad* would be an allegory, the Vālmīkian *Rāmāyana* would be an allegory, Kālidāsa's *Raghuvamsa* would be an allegory, Shakespearean Drama would be one grand allegory, Milton's *Paradise Lost* would be an allegory, Goethe's *Faust* would be an allegory, Victor Hugo's *Les Miserables* would be an allegory, Dostoyevski's *Poor Folk* would be an allegory. Literature as dealing with human passions, sentiments and emotions becomes allegorical as a matter of course! Nay, the actual life of every man and woman of flesh and blood would be an allegory. The daily incidents of world's history would be so many allegories. Human life being the theatre of contending forces necessarily becomes one perpetual allegory. The Napoleonic War was an allegory, the great armageddon of the twentieth century which we are witnessing today is an allegory; because in sooth every "Kurukshetra" represents ultimately the conflict of principles and abstract interests. To say that Rādhā-Krishna literature is such an allegory is to explain nothing. It is as much as saying that all the *dramatis personae* in these idylls stand for some attitudes of life, some conceptions of the universe, some ideas and ideals of existence. And this can be said of every person on the world's stage as of every character in art. Every individual human being is a psycho-physical complex and must carry on his or her forehead a ticket representing certain values, attributes or notions.

In the second place, can any spiritual or non-secular significance be given to these love-songs? Coomāraswāmy says in the introduction that Krishna Līlā in Brindāban is eternal, and Brindāban is the heart of man. This would be tantamount to regarding the literature as an allegory.

The following passage is taken from his Elucidations:

"Jumna bank in Vaishnava literature stands for this world regarded as the constant meeting-place of Rādhā and Krishna where amidst the affairs of daily life the soul is arrested and beguiled to her (worldly) undoing." Following this line of interpretation one would see in the parks and squares of modern cities more than what meets the ear!

In the section on "The First Passion of Krishna" we have among other things the following ecstasy of the lover about Rādhā's beauty:

"Wheresoever her twin feet fall
A lotus flower uplifts them."

To this our translator adds the note: "Thus Rādhā is very tenderly represented as divine. Every footfall finds a lotus foot-stool,—which is a constant convention of Buddhist and Hindu art. The lightness of her step is also suggested." If Rādhā is divine, every darling of every young man has ever been divine. Which mortal does not regard his sweetheart as an "angel"?

Rādhā after seeing her lover for the first time is in raptures over his heavenly grace. This is the subject matter of 'The First Passion of Rādhā.' She speaks to her friend, a girl-companion (*sakhī*):

"How can I tell the limits of my grief, my dear?
The blowing of that flute diffuses poison through my frame."

Coomāraswāmy sees in the flute of Krishna "the call of the Infinite," the "sound of the camel-bell," the "sword" of "I come to bring not peace, but a sword." Any unsophisticated reader would, however, see in all this nothing but the spell on Juliet of everything connected with Romeo. Love-fetishes and love-"charms" constitute the whole world of a young couple in love. What would not a young girl give for a "lock of hair" from her darling? Scott's poem is well known.

In the section on "Dalliance in Spring" we have the lines:

"The new young maidens, maddened with new longings,
Are hurrying to the groves.
For ever and for ever new diversions such as these
Delight the heart of Vidyāpati."

The note on "For ever and for ever" is: "Since the Krishna Līlā is eternal." Yes, because the world never becomes entirely old, and in every generation there are men and women to enjoy this "dalliance in spring."

The mood of *māna* or wilfulness is upon Rādhā. She, therefore, speaks disparagingly to her maiden-companion about her flame:

"You shall not tell me otherwise, my dear,
Little by little I came to know him better,
That Kāṇu is so cunning."

The very next remark is, however, in quite the opposite strain:

"Yet surely Kānu is good, and I am bad
Because his words beguile me."

This inconsistency on the part of the love-sick girl calls forth the following note of the translator with parallel passages from the *Prem-Sāgara*, Tāgore's *King of the Dark Chamber*, and the Irish mystic George Russell (A.E.)'s *Krishna*: "This is most typical Vaishnava poetry, in one breath blaming Krishna's wiles and proclaiming Him One without second. The note of blame is specially characteristic." The passages quoted refer of course to "Him One"! The note of blame can be very easily understood by those who know the commonplace dictum: "The course of true love never did run smooth" or "No rose without a thorn." In India at any rate every husband and every wife know what is *māna* or wilfulness. "Blowing hot and cold" in the same breath is a characteristic of the daily bickerings which sweeten and enliven the Hindu household. That *dampati-kalaha* or the civil war between the husband and the queen of the household (where "woman reigns") is "much ado about nothing," is a truism to every sane man. "The Moods of the Amorous" (*Die Laune des Verliebten*) is a pastoral drama by Goethe, his earliest extant work, in which we have an autobiographical representation of lovers' quarrels. The relation between Goethe and Kathchen is described in the following words (in Lewes' rendering) of Amine regarding her Eridon:

> "'Tis true he vexes me, and yet my sorrow pains him.
> Yet let him but reproach, begin to tease me,
> Then need I but a word, a single kind word utter,
> Away flies all his anger in a moment,
> And he will .weep with me, because he sees me weep."

Also, "The fairy link of Love thou mak'st a galling yoke.
Thou treat'st me as a slave; and I? I love thee still!"

Coomāraswāmy would not allow himself to be misunderstood. So he begins the note on this section thus: "This affection of a heroine is something compound of pride, disdain, offense and coldness: a hardening of heart. The soul's contraction though the voice of God is heard,—she will not open her doors." Is the learned Doctor really serious?

Rādhā is reproaching her lover for his infidelity and being somebody to every body:

> "By little steps I came to understand him better,
> How is his heart as fickle as the lightning.
> Forsaking the lily, he followed the screw-pine,
> Inhaling its fragrance:

But the thorns have pierced his body
His face is smeared with dust."

The translator's note is: "Here the thought approaches the prevailing motif of the *Gīta Govinda*, where Rādhā is the higher self of man, and Krishna the self-entangled in the world of sensation." This note is absurd.

Now comes the section on "Reunion after Wilfulness." It is apparent that the lovers are happy. Says Rādhā:

"My mother-in-law was asleep, and I lay in her lap,
And love-learned Kānu was lurking behind,
Bending his face to mine, how did he drink the nectar of my lips?
How often silently he laid his hand upon my breasts,
Nor let betray him any panting breath,—
My mother-in-law awoke, and Kānu ran away:
My hopes were not fulfilled, says Vidyāpati."

Evidently these lines do not require any "elucidation." Yet we have some from the translator: "Even as a wife, such dalliance before a mother-in-law would be contrary to all decorum; thus the mother-in-law represents, as it were, the cares of this world, whereby the soul is prevented from yielding herself,—and hence Vidyāpati's disappointment."

One is inclined to doubt the sanity of the annotator. The dalliance had been indulged in before the mother-in-law awoke. It could not reach the highest consummation. Hence Vidyāpati is sorry for his hero. For a girl to sleep with her mother-in-law and for the husband to steal a kiss would not be considered as impossible under conditions of rustic life in India. One should dismiss from one's mind the style of bedroom-construction prevalent in the modern West while trying to understand homelife in mediaeval Hindusthan. In any case the equation, mother-in-law=worldly cares, is absurd.

Rādhā wants to monopolize Krishna's love and asks him to avoid flirtation. A very simple wish and a very simple command. Her words are:

"And take no other maiden on your lap
Then I will speak of love with you."

Our annotator explains this legitimate "jealousy" thus: "Rādhā presumptuously claims for herself alone the love that is given to all that seek." No man of commonsense is likely to swallow this interpretation.

The section on "Reproaches, Lack and Longing" begins with the following note: "The departure of Krishna to Mathurā is God forsaking the soul or seeming to do so; the complaint of Rādhā is. "Why hast thou forsaken me?" Every man who has to absent himself from his wife or sweetheart is then a God! In fact, where is the girl of human parents born who has not, in her longing for the separated lover, conceived him as the very God of her soul, the core of her being, the life of her life, and so on?

The lovers have been separated for sometime. The pangs of separation are being deeply felt on both sides. The longing of Rādhā at times takes the form of a reverie when she considers herself identified with her darling. This is not a very extraordinary phenomenon in the world of lovers. Even in Wordsworth we have "the Reverie of Poor Susan," who sees in her vision "the one only dwelling on earth that she loves."

The condition of Rādhā pining away and longing for her darling is thus described by a companion:

"Often in meditation on the name of Mādhava,
She changes into Mādhava himself:
Forgetful of her own desires and of her own identity
She is enamoured of her own charms.

* * *

The cry of Rādhā, Rādhā, echoing repeatedly,

* * *

When she is with Rādhā, she thinks that she is with Mādhava,
And when with Mādhava, Rādhā."

Allowing for the hyperbole of poetry, one may be allowed to remark that unless a man or woman were to have more or less of this experience of identity with the beloved while they are apart, one would doubt the sincerity and depth of their love. In the present instance where Rādhā's attachment to her darling is AI, there is nothing to wonder at. Yet Dr. Coomāraswāmy drags in the ideas of God, Divine Union, etc. The note is given below:

"This is one of the most obviously mystical of Vidyāpati's songs: 'I am he whom I love, and he whom I love is I'—Mansur Hallaj. cf. the exclamation *Shivoham*, 'Shiva is myself' (*Sohambhāva*, he being I); and the injunction *Devo bhutvā devam yajet*, 'By becoming God, worship Him!" According to our annotator, then, every young lady who has the name-fetish and other fetishes regarding her lover or husband would be a worshipper of God. Of course the lover is the

the whole world, God, and what-not to his darling, but not in the same way as Coomāraswāmy would have us believe about Rādhā. Wilhelm's mind is thus described by Goethe in his *Wilhelm Meister's Apprenticeship* (Carlyle's translation): "She, too, hears these flutes. She feels whose remembrance, whose love of her it is that makes the night full of music. In distance even we are united by these melodies; as in every separation by the ethereal accordance of love. Ah! two hearts that love each other are as two magnetic needles. Whatever moves the one must move the other along with it; for it is one power that works in both, one principle that pervades them. How often when absent from her and lost in thoughts about her, happening to touch a book, a piece of dress, of aught else have I thought I felt her hand, so entirely was I invested with her presence!"

If Rādhā's eyes, ears, memories and visions are to be treated as something superhuman, Scott is also speaking of superhuman sense-organs in the following lines:

> "O lovers' eyes are sharp to see,
> And lovers' eyes in hearing;
> And love, in life's extremity,
> Can lend an hour of cheering."

Or, when somebody says

> "That same low voice across my garden aisles
> Might not have reached my ear for wind or bird.
> But it has spoken across a thousand miles,
> And I have heard!"——

are we not to understand that these are the words of a soul rapt in "meditation"? The life of heart-beats and agitated brain, the life of memories of and longings for the loved one, the life of flights on imagination's wings, the life of love-concentrated face and steadfast eyes, the life of "sweet unrest,"—has always uttered itself in the language of *dhyāna* or meditation, in vocabulary divine. And yet nobody would consider a modern love-sick girl as a "seer," a "Rishi" or a devout nun in the sense known to theologists. But she *is* a "seer" and a devotee in her own way and believes herself to be such. The Rādhā of Vidyāpati is nothing more than this, a maiden in love's spell.

There is thus nothing "most obviously mystical" in the following modern lines which may stand as the autobigraphy of a Rādhā in reverie:

"Would you understand
The language with no word,
The speech of brook and bird
Of waves along the sand?
Would you make your own
The meaning of the leaves,
The song the silence weaves
Where little winds make moan?
Would you know how sweet
The falling of the rill
The calling of the hill
All tunes the days repeat?"

The experiences of Vidyāpati's Rādhā were no other than what are suggested in these questions. And what is, after all, the "mystery" here?

"The secret of the ear
Is in the open heart."

Lovers with "open heart" will always know their

dreamy self-forgetfulness in terms of contemplation, meditation, *dhyāna*, *yoga*. Any other description would be a sacrilege and a profanation. Call these sentiments "most obviously mystical" if you like.

Our Rādhā has been a revolutionist. She has transgressed the conventional morality of her surroundings. She has given up her folk and family, so to speak, in yielding to the idol of her dream. So at times she criticizes herself. There is a note of self-reproach as can be easily guessed:

> "How many reproaches and scornful words of my elders
> I counted for naught in my heart, deepladen in love,
> For whose sake I forsook without shame the path of duty,
> He now has forsaken my companionship."

This conflict between love and duty is also the theme of Tāgore's *Chitrā*. We have seen how the greatest of all warriors, Arjuna, the proud hero with a profound mission, succumbed to "the one woman" at the very first sight. That was a triumph of sex over Bushidō or Kshatriyaism—"an imperfection which yet is noble and grand."

Coomāraswāmy, however, interprets Rādhā's attitude thus: "The idea of reproach is essential to the drama of the soul, and a leading motif of the greater part of Rādhā-Krishna literature." He quotes a few parallel passages with spiritual significance, of which the following is from the Bible: "Blessed are ye when man shall revile and persecute you for My sake." He might as well have quoted the statements of every martyr and revolutionist in world's history.

He emphasises the spiritual idea thus: "To understand the necessity and significance of *reproach*, is to comprehend how it was not merely possible but inevitable that in a society where the strictest possible conception of woman's honour prevails, the self-surrender of Rādhā should be regarded as the natural symbol of the soul's self-gift to God." Tāgore's Arjuna forgetting his mission is the exact counterpart of Rādhā's being a wanton. Is Arjuna also an allegory?

Krishna is describing his lonesomeness at Mathurā where he has perforce to be without his darling. But not a moment of his life is he without his Rādhā in imagination. Rādhā is the world in which he lives—the centre of his dreams. So he has to state to a friend of Rādhā's:

> "Beside another love in regal state,
> I live like any anchorite."

He is so absorbed in his own Rādhā that the "regal state" at Mathurā is no more than a shadow and does not influence his life at all. But our annotator wants us to "understand by this the loneliness of God in heaven, lacking the love of men." Every lover separated from his sweetheart is certainly a lonesome God, but he lacks only the love of "the one woman," of one little heart which he worships.

The last section of these idylls is called "Reunion and the Flow of Nectar." Everybody knows of the anticipations of meeting the beloved after long separation. Rādhā also like any girl of flesh and blood is rehearsing within herself as to how she will meet Kānu, what will be her first words, what should be her dress, and so forth. In fact, she is counting days, hours, minutes. Only one word is her encyclopaedia, viz., "Krishna."

"When Hari comes to Gokula town,
I shall give my necklace of pearls for festal knots,
And my heavy breasts as festal urns.
I shall offer my nipples as sprouts of the scented mango,
In Mādhava's service I shall achieve my heart's desires."

Any loving girl would think and dream: "My darling and I shall then live together forever. I shall love and serve him for ever and for ever. There will be no more parting in silence and tears. Every wish I shall read from his eyes. Nothing would be too much for me. And I believe my dearest sweetheart also is probably thinking and dreaming like myself."

Coomāraswāmy, however, gives this "elucidation": "Rādhā has learnt at last that service is self-realisation and self-expression." I wonder if people would not regard this as caricature.

Rādhā has met her lover after long. Her joy knows no bounds, is really too deep for words. Her whole world has come back to her—she feels a new life, "the glory and freshness of a dream." She is, therefore, talking in superlatives and hyperboles:

"How shall I tell of my boundless joy, my dear,—
Mādhava abiding day after day in my house?—
A shawl in the winter is my beloved, a gentle breeze in the summer,
My dear is a shelter from the storm, and a boat on the river."

One might say that here is no hyperbole at all. And

yet Coomāraswāmy must add the following note: "The 'boat on the river' goes back to the oldest Buddhist idea of a raft or boat wherein to cross the *samsāra*, the sea of this world, to reach the further shore; just as in the carol 'Come over the burn, Besse,' 'The burne is this world blind'!"

Rādhā is giving her darling thousand and one terms of endearment and yet feels that language is too poor to describe what he is to her:

> "A mirror in hand, a flower in my hair,
> Surm of my eyes, tambul of my mouth,
> Musk on my breast, a necklace about my throat,
> All the gear on my body, the life of my house.
> Life of my life—I know Thou art these—
> But tell me, O Mādhava, what art Thou in sooth?
> Avers Vidyāpati—Each is both."

Our annotator answers this love-jubilant, over-joyed lass in the following note: "Rādhā feels that Krishna whom she had thought her equal, is indeed beyond her ken, but the poet answers, 'That art Thou,' proclaiming their Unity." Yes, because the darling and the lover are "one soul in bodies two," as Shelley has declared.

Coomāraswāmy now points out the song "which throws a light upon the whole wreath of songs," the *Padābalī* of Vidyāpati. It is too well known:

> "What would you ask of my feelings, my dear,—
> From the day of my birth I have seen His beauty,
> And yet are my eyes unsatisfied:
> My ears have continually heard His honeyed speech,
> But I have not attained the path of audition.
> Many a night have I passed in play,

And never have learnt what is dalliance :
Myriad aeons I held Him close to my heart,
And yet no rest has reached that heart.
Vidyāpati says : For your heart's ease
You have met with One who is non-pareil."

In this bit of joyous effusion there is virtually no hyperbole except in the phrases "from the day of birth," and "myriad aeons." The whole is perfectly clear, intelligible and natural. Coomāraswāmy, however, explains this unbounded joy of a love-fed heart in the following way : "The soul perceives that she had ears to hear and eyes to see ever since she came to birth, yet she has neither heard nor seen ; and now she cannot have enough of hearing and seeing." Readers, however, would remember Tennyson's line : "I do not understand, I love." Every person under love's spell must admit this. The "magic circle" of love keeps men and women dumbfounded, paralysed, confused. Tāgore's Arjuna never recovered from this love-spell. Even towards the end of the poem, the proud "world-conqueror" had to confess to Chitrā : "I never seem to know you aright. You seem to me like a goddess hidden within a golden image. I cannot touch you, I cannot pay you my dues in return for your priceless gifts." And when Chitrā gave the simple reply : "The gift that I proudly bring you is the heart of a woman," did Arjuna understand her? He had absolutely no word—he was amazed in "her charmed sphere." And if he could collect any words, he would have said "I do not understand, I love." In fact, this is the significance of the pithy last line : "Beloved, my life is full." And if Arjuna is an allegory, because as has been suggested above, every person is an allegory, it is the allegory of the triumph of the heart of a woman. It is impossible likewise to see any other allegory in the whole Rādhā-Krishna literature.

It is impossible to find a single song among the one hundred and thirtyeight in Coomāraswāmy's English about which it can be said: "It is quite certain that many poems of Vidyāpati have an almost wholly spiritual significance." All are absolutely secular.

The learned Doctor is not blind to the secular or carnal element in these love-songs. In fact, he has taken Tāgore's following lines to be the keynote of the *Padābalī*:

> "My passion shall burn as the flame of Salvation,
> The flower of my love shall become the ripe
> fruit of Devotion."

But he seems to take this "passion" as almost a necessary "evil". His "Introduction" is meant principally to offer an apology for Vidyāpati's sensuousness and extollation of human desires. Coomāraswāmy would have been very happy if he could interpret the whole Rādhā-Krishna literature as an expression of spiritual or Godward love. But the earthly element, the physical beauty, the "dirt," "the dust," the "imperfection," "the heart of a woman," the human love, the pleasures of sense, are too many to be ignored. Really, it is impossible to recognise any other pleasures in the world of Vidyāpati. Coomāraswāmy feels this and has tried to whitewash it according to his ideas of Hindu morality, Hindu standard of domestic decorum, and Hindu traditional interpretation of Vaishnava thought. The attempt has been a huge failure and has imparted to his introduction and elucidation an air of duplicity and insincerity.

The one fallacy which is responsible for this dualism and inconsistency of the veteran philosopher-poet-critic consists in his persistent refusal, even in spite of himself, to admit the fact that it is sex and nothing but sex that supplies the motif of Vidyāpati's art. And sex does not require any apology. It can stand on its own dignity—"an imperfection which yet is noble and grand."

V. THE BOILING-POINT OF LOVE-HEAT.

The Idylls of Rādhā do not require any elucidation. They are written in the language whose alphabet is known to the "open heart." Some of the conceits and images of Indian rustic life and folk-art, however, may not be easily appreciated by foreigners. But everybody would feel that the whole pastoral is an encyclopaedic idyll of love-tonics, love-fetishes, love-charms and aphrodisiacs. Vidyāpati is a student of sex, a professor of *Kāma-shāstra* or erotics, a researcher into the ins and outs of sense-life. His Rādhā-Krishna songs are nothing but erotics idealized—studies in the *ādi*, (i.e., primal and fundamental) or *shringāra* (i.e., amorous) *rasa* (i.e., emotion, passion), one of the nine according to Hindu Aesthetics.

Vidyāpati has specialized in this branch of Hindu art, he is a specialist in sex-studies. His strength and weakness are the strength and weakness of all specialists. Specialists can at best give us "the truth and nothing but the truth," but not "the whole truth." Vidyāpati also has given us "the truth and nothing but the truth," but not "the whole truth," not the only truth. *Shrin-*

gāra rasa is a truth, and nothing but the truth, but not the whole truth, not the only truth. If Vidyāpati requires any defence at all, it is this.

Charles Lamb in his celebrated defence of the Restoration Drama made a significant remark: "The standard of police is not the standard of poetical justice." This defence has virtually been a condemnation.

Schiller, the great prophet of *Sturm und drang* creed, also considers the disregard of conventional morality by artists as perfectly justifiable:

"The laws of propriety are foreign to innocent nature; only the experience of corruption has given origin to them. But as soon as that corruption has taken place and natural innocence has vanished from manners, the laws of propriety are sacred. But the very thing which constitutes the poet is that he banishes from himself everything which reminds him of an artificial world, that he may restore nature in her primitive simplicity. And if he has done this, he is thereby absolved from all laws by which a perverted heart seeks security against itself. * * * If thou who readest and hearest him art no longer innocent, and if thou canst not even momentarily become so by his purifying presence, it is thy *misfortune*, and not his; thou forsakest him, he did not sing for thee."

This defence of immorality, coming as it does from the author of the *Robbers*, the apostle of Romanticism, would suit the citizens (?) of Rousseau's "State of Nature," but can never be swallowed by people living in organized societies who are bound to respect "codes" and conventions.

My attitude with regard to Vidyāpati is quite different. He does not require any defence at all. He is a "specialist," and we do not go to a specialist for "the whole duty of man."

Vidyāpati's love is not an industrialized commodity, not a factor that is being utilized by "Breeders' Associations," not a thing for divorce-legislation, not the topic for a John Stuart Mill's *Subjection of Women.* Vidyāpati's love is the steam generated without a steam-engine—the "power" not yet harnessed to the exigencies of social needs. Vidyāpati's love is the Niagara Falls or Himālayan Pāglā Jhorā waiting to be transformed by a dynamo,—the Kāl Vaisākhī of Bengal or the Indian Monsoon,—the Ocean Pacific in winter,—the "wild West Wind"—the "Thou, O uncontrollable." Vidyāpati's love is an element among the elements; an energy of Nature, a cosmic force, a "noumenal" principle, the very spirit of Love, the relation between Purusha and Prakriti. Vidyāpati's love is love "in vacuum," "unconditioned" love, love without the perspective of time and space, love as "the-thing-in-itself."

The synthesis of sex and spirit, the secular and the non-secular, can be realized not by insulting the sex and the secular but by giving them their dues, by recognising the dignity of the sex and the dignity of the secular. That synthesis may not be the motif of every piece of art in every generation; but where the dignity of the sex or the dignity of the secular has been the special motif, we must not obtrude altogether alien and extraneous considerations while trying to appreciate that. *Chitrā* is a specialization in sex, *Padābali* is a specialization in sex, *Vikramorvasie* is a specialization in sex. Their "criticism of life" is embodied in the following two equations: Sex-desire=love, and Love=sex-desire. The artists may be believed to have been adding after this line: "And this is all ye know on earth and need to know." Our rejoinder then would be—"True, deeply true, and we have great need to know it. But this is only a truth and nothing but the truth, but not the whole truth. You are specialists in *shringāra rasa,* all the other eight rasas you have not touched. Therefore your equations are partial, your criticism of life is 'hypothetical'." The dignity of the sex can be maintained only by this attitude and not by converting human love with all its warmth and glow into a faint echo of something transcendental or by regarding the joys of the flesh as only an allegory of the "Beatific Vision."

Love "in vacuum" is the topic for one class of studies, love under conditions of time and space is the topic for another. If, therefore, the "whole duty of man" is to be sought, let us come to the *Raghu-vamsam* ("The House of Raghu") for the Vikramādityan Napoleonic India, to the *Rāmāyana* of Tulsi Dāsa and Krittivāsa for Mediaeval Hindusthan, and works like the *Ānanda-matha* ("The Abbey of Bliss") of Bankimchandra Chatterji for the Young India of today. In the meantime we have no right to interpret Chitrā, Rādhā and Urvasie in accordance with the conventional ideas of Hindu decorum or Indian domestic morality.

Vidyāpati, as the poet of "absolute" love, of love as a passion among passions, of love as an elemental motive power, is not exclusively an Indian poet, but the poet of all mankind. Vidyāpati is a world's artist—probably the greatest artist in his line. As a study in sex, the *Padābalī* is the world's greatest classic. We see here nothing national or local—it is all human, universal. Vidyāpati has, like Shakespeare, "held the mirror up to nature" in his own way. Men and women in every age and every clime will read in it the story of their sex-life.

There is no Oriental love, and there is no Occidental love. Love as the thing in itself is ever the same. The love of the most barbarous boor, the love of the most polished society-girl, the love of the Scythian, the love of the Negro, the love of the Caledonian, and the love of the people brought up between theatres and "variety-houses" would never differ in origin or in nature. Vidyāpati would thus "soothe the love-laden soul" of the innocent maiden born between mountains and valleys as of the University-trained women.

It may be asked "What are the special claims of Vidyāpati to our recognition?" The answer is: None. We do not come to Vidyāpati for anything special. Passages may be quoted from the literature of every people which would show that Vidyāpati has not given us anything which others have not conceived or anything which others cannot easily perceive.

> "These are really the thoughts of all men in all
> ages and lands......
> This is the grass that grows wherever the land
> is and the water is,
> This is the common air that bathes the globe."

But we may ransack the whole love-literature of the world to find out another thorough and comprehensive specialist in this subject, and we shall search in vain. The whole career of love, the birth, growth and development of the sex-impulse, the normal and abnormal manifestations of the great passion, the biography or rather auto-biography of Eros or Madana Himself, have been perpetuated for the human race in about one thousand (according to up-to-date collection) love-lyrics by this great student of human nature in mediaeval India.

Vidyāpati has given us a complete psychology of love with also the diagnosis and pathology of the love-sick. Like a student of experimental psychology in a modern philosophical laboratory, our Vidyāpati seems to have approached the human heart with stethoscopes and all the statistical and mechanical apparatus known in his days. He seems to have held the pulse of the lover and counted its throbbings. He seems to have photographed the rise and fall of the breast, and registered the calculus of pleasures and pains under varying conditions of love-stimuli. He seems to have measured the heat and glow of face and numbered the heart-beats and lip-quiverings according to the changes in the atmosphere of passions. In his cinematograph we view the successive phases of two young souls in love. The heart of a woman and the heart of a man would always be gratified to see their likenesses in this Hindu artist's pictures. Neither the story of Dante's fascination for Beatrice in his *Vita Nuova* ("The New Life") nor the portraiture of lovers' moods in Goethe's pastoral, *Die Laune des Verliebten*, nor the sonnets of Shakespeare nor those of Rossetti in the *House of Life* can replace Vidyāpati's *Padābalī*.

Coomāraswāmy has said that Vidyāpati is a "mystic Burns." But what is Burns worth if he is not a mystic? He is not Alexander Pope, the poet of classic restraint and conventional morals. Roby Burns is the herald of "abandon," of divine madness, of response to the impulses of nature, of self-forgetfulness and ecstasy, of freedom of soul, of the vision of a new life, the only "real" life. If Burns is not a mystic, Vidyāpati is not.

The fallacy consists first in treating Vidyāpati as an allegorist, i.e., as a religious poet speaking through the medium of secular passions, and secondly, in taking mysticism exclusively in connexion with religious phenomena or spiritual experiences, e.g., those of rosicrucians. Vidyāpati is not an allegorist, and yet he is a mystic, if mystic anybody ever was. Burns has not dabbled in the religious or spiritual experiences; and yet he is a mystic, if mystic anybody ever was.

What then is mysticism? Mysticism is an attitude of mind, an angle of vision, a standpoint of life, a method of outlook on the unverse. But every attitude gives rise to its own values, every angle creates its own picture, every standpoint its own panorama, every method yields its own results. Mysticism is thus also a system of values, a *kakemono* of panoramas and landscapes, a body of truths.

Once you are a mystic you have that methodology and that philosophy, that attitude and that body of truths. There is no oriental mysticism, there is no occidental mysticism. Mysticism is mysticism as water is H_2O. At the equator and at the poles, in the depth of the mines and in the height of the mountains water is water. There is no torrid zone water and no polarregion water. So mysticism as an attitude and as a philosophy is universal, is human. The mediaeval mystics of Europe and Asia are the same as the mystics of the primitive world or of the modern times.

If I may use a common scientific notion, I may state that "under certain conditions of temperature and pressure" human intellect or the brain of man produces the phenomenon with the mystical method and mystical philosophy. Wherever you find those conditions you are bound to have mystics and mysticism. The world's ingredients under certain conditions of temperature and pressure must produce that phenomenon called H_2O. So mysticism is neither the product of Hindu brain, nor the product of Saracenic brain, nor the product of Christian brain, nor the product of Chinese brain. It is "inevitable" under certain conditions, be they in the East or in the West.

Rossetti sings of the "Sea-limits:"

"Consider the Sea's listless chime:
Time's self it is, made audible,—
The murmur of the earth's own shell,

* * *

As the world's heart of rest and wrath,
Its painful pulse is in the sands.

* * *

Gather a shell from the strewn beach
And listen at its lips: they sigh
The same desire and mystery,
The echo of the whole sea's speech.
And all mankind is thus at heart
Not anything but what thou art;
And, Earth, Sea, Man are all in each."

Nicholson writes:

"I find you in the wild unpeopled places,
Where mile on mile the heatherland unrolls

You smile in simple upturned flower-faces
With honest yellow sunlight aureoles!
The curlews crying on the windy moors
The glad larks singing in the blue have souls
Star-clear as yours!
I find you best, I think, beside the sea,
It breathes your very spirit—fresh and clean,
Yet full of breath and light and mystery
Deepness on deepness, hidden and unseen!
In the untramell'd tide you are expressed
So well and warmly! Sea and sky between
I find you best."

Do these differ from the following (in my rendering) by Tāgore?

"E'er and oft do Thy melodies vibrate
Deep in the grove of mine innermost being;
Ever and oft is Thy throne resplendent
Wide on my beauteous lotus of heart.
By the odours of Thine avalon charm'd
Does my soul sojourn in this lovely earth;
Ever and oft with the dusts of Thy feet
Do I deck my limbs for garment's sake.
The skies throughout do I find unobscur'd
The ruling presence of Thy silent smile;
Ever and oft do all vanities mine
Before Thy glories recoil guilty 'sham'd.
Discords vanish at Thy propitious call,
Through Thy music comes grace o'er heart and all."

How, again, does the mysticism of the neo-Platonist Plotinus of the third century A.D. differ from that of the Chinese Tāoists or Hindu Vedāntists? "The spiritual ambition of Plotinus was not to be satisfied," says Webb in his *History of Philosophy*, "by sympathy with the universal life, nor yet by the contemplation of the eternal Intelligence. He sought, and was believed by his friends on several occasions to have attained, a union with the ultimate principle, the highest God of all...... Union with the highest can be attained only in a state in which all sense of distinction is lost, a state of ecstasy or rapture." This is nothing short of Indian *Yoga*, the monism of Hindu thinkers, of whom a recent representative was Vivek-ānanda.

Take the following from Chuangtsze, the Chinese mystic of the fourth century B.C.: "Be free yourself from subjective ignorance and individual peculiarities, find the universal Tāo in your own being, and you will be able to find it in others, too, because the Tāo cannot be one in one thing and another in another. The Tāo must be the same in every existence, because 'I' and the 'ten thousand beings' grow from the selfsame source, and in this oneness of things we can bury all our opinions and contradictions." The extract is from Suzuki's *History of Chinese Philosophy*.

The Sufism of mediaeval Persia, the Zen (*dhyān*)-ism of mediaeval Japan, the Yogaism of Mediaeval India, the transcendentalism or romanticism of Young Germany, and Carlylean mysticism, are all birds of a feather. They may differ only in the emphasis laid on certain incidents or particulars, but have a family likeness. Just as love is one and the same all the world over, so is mysticism one and the same everywhere. It is a certain type of mentality and may flourish in any part of the globe.

Burns is a mystic because he has the Sufi temperament, because he has the Herderian or Fichtean temperaent, because he has the Carlylean temperament, the temperament of the Tāoists, Vedāntists and Zenists. The same wings which carry a Schelling, an Omar Khayyam, a Kabīr, or a Mazzini carry also the folk-poet of Caledonia. A common vision inspires them all—but their message they deliver in diverse forms. They express themselves in different ways and lay stress on different particulars. We have thus an educational mystic, a political mystic, a philosophical mystic, a religious mystic, and so on. But they have all drunk of the same fountain of inner self, the spirit, the subjective consciousness, the untouchable, the infinite, the perennial springs of Nature and Life, the eternal "realities" of the universe, the world's permanent verities.

The following is the *Gītā* of Roby Burns:

"Oh! what is death but parting breath?—
On many a bloody plain
I've dared his face, and in this place
I scorn him yet again!
Untie these bands from off my hands,
And bring to me my sword!
And there's no man in all Scotland
But I will brave him at a word.
Now farewell light, thou sunshine bright,
And all beneath the sky!
May coward shame disdain his name,
The wretch that dares not die!"

Human life produces the same phenomenon under the same conditions of temperature and pressure. There is no Scotch mentality and no Hindu mentality. Tegh

Bāhādur, the Sikh martyr of mediaeval India, might have uttered these very words. "Macpherson's Farewell" is really the farewell of the Macphersons of all mankind.

Burns is a mystic because he sings of infinite bliss, of eternal sunshine, of the "light that never was on sea or land," of perpetual *Phālgunis*, of a new world of bursting vital life. His were the cry of the poor and the cry of the slave. He is one of the world's first socialists. In the "Highland Widow's Lament" we have a deeper sense of humanity, a widening of the world's horizon, and a reverence for human passion and character, which can be experienced only on imagination's wings, as an "ethereal minstrel," and not from the convention-rooted platform of this lowly ground. A vision from that height is the vision of a mystic.

"I was the happiest of a'the clan,
Sair, sair may I repine;
For Donald was the bravest man
And Donald he was mine.
Till Charlie Stewart came at last,
Sae far to set us free;
My Donald's arm was wanted then
For Scotland and for me.
Their woefu' fate what need I tell,
Right to the wrang did yield:
My Donald and his country fell
Upon Culloden field."

Burns is a mystic, because he lives on the furthest verge of emotions. His life in intense, he is an extremist. And from that extreme of world's horizon he catches a glimpse of the unknown, the hereafter, and the twilight of a nebulous new sun. He is a mystic because he can sacrifice everything at the altar of his feeling. With Byronic fever and enthusiasm he can die for his ideal.

Burns had been the seer of pre-Raphaelitism half a century before it was officially declared. He is the precursor of Turner and Burne-Jones, of Ruskin and Morris, as the idealizer of the fresher aspects of nature and life. He can live visionary hours with a Wordsworth's cuckoo, converting the earth we pace into "an unsubstantial faery place." He is a Rossetti of the unlettered folk, and can realize in his unsophisticated way how—

> "Heaven holds breath and hears
> The beating heart of Love's own breast."

What else is Vidyāpati? Are not the following also the words of Rādhā?

> "When I sleep I dream,
> When I wauk I'm eerie,
> Sleep I can get nane
> For thinking on my dearie."

Burns' supreme wish is given below:

> "Let fortune's gifts at random flee,
> They never shall draw a wish froe me,
> Supremely blest in love and thee,
> In the birks of Aberfeldy."

This supreme bliss, this ecstasy, this "short story of a perfect moment that has neither past nor future," is not to be understood by everybody but only by the "initiates," and is therefore the vision of a mystic. It is too intense, too hot, too impetuous for the worldlywise, for the bread-and-butter philosophers, for the utilitarians.

It is intensity that constitutes a great part of mysticism. It is fervour that makes people mystical. Mysticism is the philosophy of a brain all aglow, of a soul in flames, of emotion at the boiling-point. The same thing in social phenomena would be called revolutionism or anarchism, in art and literature would be called idealism or romanticism, in religion and spiritual experiences would be called transcendentalism or mysticism. So many terms express but one idea, viz., the passion in ebullition.

Vidyāpati is not a greater idealist then Burns. Burns is not less mystical than Vidyāpati. Mysticism is not the monopoly of the Hindu mediaevals. Idealism is not the monopoly of the European romanticists. There is a Burns-element in Hindu life, and there is a Vidyāpati-element in Eur-American life. You will see that element only "under certain conditions of temperature and pressure."

"Little pot, soon hot" used to be said about Shelley. But we are not concerned at present with "too little" or "too soon," we are concerned with the heat. We want to know only the temperature. The remark gives us Shelley as human life at the boiling-point, and we accept this as true. The boiling-point varies with varying conditions—with the ranges of height above the sea-level. We need recognise these varying conditions while explaining the caloric of emotion in each instance. For from the dead level of Pope's cold swinish materialism to the height of Shelley's fine frenzy and Whitman's glowing enthusiasm we can have a graduated scale of literary thermometer. And this scale is not for the British-American art-world alone, it can be used as a scale for measuring the art-heat, the emotion-heat, the life's intensity, the passion's glow, the love's caloric, of all races and all ages. It will evaluate and "standardize" the world's literary treasures and find out the Popes, the Blakes, the Burnses, the Wordsworths, the Byrons, the Schillers, the Klingers, the Shelleys, the Chateaubriands, the La Martines, the Victor Hugos, the Rossettis, the Brownings, and Whitmans, of the human race.

The atmosphere that Vidyāpati breathes is the atmosphere of Shelley, or the Italian atmosphere of Rossetti, the prophet of pre-Raphaelitism. He is the poet of passion at the boiling point. His Rādhā and Krishna are boiling-point creations. And the boiling-point creations of any poet of the world would be brothers and sisters to the Hindu Krishna and Rādhā. Like Romeo and Juliet, these creations of Indian art stand as norms of sex-life's intensity. There is nothing local or national or Indian or Hindu or mediaeval in Vidyāpati's Rādhā and Krishna. Vidyāpati dwells above the snow-line where the mountain peaks are ever capped with snow. All dwellers above the snowline are his kin. The Alpine heights, the Rocky heights and the Himālayan heights present, beyond a certain level, the same panorama of "eternal sunshine" and of.

"Peaks where the lilies tremble against the snow,
Far bleak crags, with their lights that every hour
Change, till the fire dies from the sun's last glow."

Souls all ablaze must, like the snow-capped hill-tops of Asia, Europe, Africa and America, be cognates with a family-likeness wheresoever they be born. Imagination and Art above snowline must be uniform.

The kinship of world's idealists and mystics is very well

expressed by the American Shelley, Walt Whitman, who was "a rebel in his message" and "a rebel in his art:"

> This moment yearning and thoughtful sitting alone,
> It seems to me there are other men in other lands yearning and thoughtful,
> It seems to me I can look over and behold them in Germany, Italy, France, Spain,
> Or far, far away, in China, or in Russia or Japan, talking other dialects,
> And it seems to me if I could know these men I should become attached to them as I do to men in my own lands,
> O I know we should be brethren and lovers,
> I know I should be happy with them."

The Vidyāpatis, Rossettis, Whitmans and Schillers of the world would thus know one other at first glance, because they have been forged into shape and being at the same anvil under the same thermal energy.

Vidyāpati is not a Hindu, nor is Whitman a Yankee so long as they are idealists or mystics, i.e., souls in flames. Let us feel a bit of this American spark:

> "O hymen, O hymenee! Why do you tantalise me thus?
> O why sting me for a swift moment only?
> Why can you not continue? O why do you now cease?
> Is it because if you continued beyond the swift moment you would soon certainly kill me?"

Again, "I am he that aches with amorous love;

> Does the earth gravitate? does not all matter, aching, attract all matter?
> So the body of me to all I meet or know."

Vidyāpati is the Shelley of this "amorous love." The *Padābalī* is ablaze at the boiling-point of love's heat. We notice here the convection-currents which set in along with the ebullition of feeling under the magic wand of Madana. Shelley, however, is more comprehensive, more sweeping than Vidyāpati. Shelley's heat consumes the whole world of man's activities and thoughts. Shelley is Revolution in all its branches—the "wild West Wind" of every passion. Vidyāpati covers a very small ground. He is the Shelley of only "the heart of a woman," the Whitman or Rossetti of a single *rasa,* the singer, pure and simple, of the dignity of sex-function, of the joys and griefs of carnal life, the idealizer of mighty sexual impulse on the lines, so to speak, of Morris' Chaucerian romantic tales in the *Earthly Paradise.*

VI. THE DIGNITY OF SEX.

The "Everlasting Nay" of Positivism is the *ultima thule* of world-culture in every stage of its history. But the mystery of one generation becomes a truism of the next. The *ultima thules* are vanishing every decade—poetry giving way to plain prose, romance to solid facts, scepticism to science. Human brain is ever depriving the eternal world of ideals of its treasures.

Religion has thus been driven out of its citadel of romance and mystery. We no longer approach the mysteries of religious experience from the top coming downwards, we begin with them at the bottom and proceed upwards. We commence our studies in religion with anthropology and end in psychology. We do not again expatiate on the metaphysics of the soul before we have done some laboratory work in experimental psychology.

The Bastille of Love also is being similarly bombarded by the advance guard of conquering positivism. The mystery and romance of Love are fast disappearing before our eyes. Even six decades ago Whitman was misunderstood when he published the following lines in *The Leaves of Grass*:

> "A woman waits for me, she contains all, nothing is lacking,
> Yet all were lacking, if sex were lacking, or if the moisture of the right man were lacking.
> Sex contains all, bodies, souls,
> Meanings, proofs, purities, delicacies, results, promulgations,
> Songs, commands, health, pride, the maternal mystery, the seminal milk,
> All hopes, benefactions, bestowals, all the passions, loves, beauties, delights of the earth,
> All the governments, judges, gods, follow'd persons of the earth,
> These are contained in sex as parts of itself, and justifications of itself."

This was certainly mystical, vague, "mere words," if not the prelude to a shamelessly outspoken glorification of sex-life. It was in truth a profanation, because love was then sacred and sex a mystery.

But today sex is not so great a mystery. Sex is already a problem among problems. Sex has entered the industrial arena. Sex is a political shibboleth. Sex is encroaching on the University Campus. And with the problem has been born the science. Sex is a growing science. And with the science have come experiments. There are the Mendelists, the Eugenists, the plant-breeders, the "sterilizers" and so forth. The magic of sex is retiring into the limbo of oblivion never to make its appearance again. Sex is no more to be an "Everlasting Nay," the despair of philosophers, poets and statesmen.

It is at this stage of world's evolution that Kālidāsa has been reborn in Aurobinda Ghosh's *Hero and the Nymph,* Vidyāpati in Coomāraswāmy's *Bangīya Padābalī,* and an episode of the *Mahābhārata* in Tāgore's *Chitrā.* This is, as it were, the rebirth of Aristotle in Bacon, the *re*-presentation of Plutarch in Shakespeare—the awakening of Greece after a slumber of one millennium. Hindu "humanism" revived is a vital force not only of the Renaissance in Young India, but has also a message for the neo-romanticists and neo-positivists of the whole world.

(a) *Sex-element in Hindu Culture.*

Humanism in India as in Classical Hellas and in the modern West has ever been an expression of all-round secularism or positivism; and of this humanism sex-interest has been a great part. The sex-element is as important a factor in Hindu Culture as the folk-element; and both have yet to be given their dues by students of Indology.

Sex has been a principal motif of Hindu literature and art. Sex has ever occupied a powerful position in the formation of religious precepts and practices. And the sex-idea has been prominent also in domestic life and social institutions. The sex-factor may be said to enter as a conception in every socio-religious item. The Rādhā-Krishna songs of Vidyāpati have thus a background, context or *milieu*, sufficiently wide and varied not only in India's art and literature (e.g., *Purānas* and *Tantras*) but also in the incidents of its daily existence.

Worship of *lingam* or phallus as the creative male element is too deep-rooted in Hindu consciousness to be treated as an aberration. Nor is the male sex deified only in its generative function. Shiva, the "Great God," stands for the thousand and one functions and aspects of the male principle, both beneficent and malevolent. If the Hindu knows one Krishna to be a lover and a sweetheart, he knows another Krishna as a statesman and a warrior. And there are the ideal husband, the ideal father, the ideal brother, the ideal ruler, and so forth, in the Rāma-stories.

Deification and extollation of the female element have been none the less prominent. If Rādhā is a sweetheart and a darling, Kālī is the inspirer of a Perseus the Deliverer, or of an Andreas Hofer, e.g., a Pratāp-āditya or a Shivāji. If Rādhā enlivens maidenhood and young age, Sītā and Sāvitrī are the idols of *hausfraus*' daily life. The female sex as the embodiment of *shakti* or energy has been really accorded the highest and most comprehensive place in Hindu socio-religious polity.

Most of the functions which have to be observed in Indian everyday life have a sex-reference. It is this sex-element which sweetens and enriches and diversifies the dull monotony of existence. Even the little incidents of the *punya pukur* or "miniature-tank"-worship performed by Hindu girls before marriage are adapted to the growing sex-consciousness about the age of pubescence. The Rāma-legends and Shiva-legends are as full of such romantic little episodes as the Rādhā-Krishna stories, and these stories are no mere library-studies but are integral parts of life. And among the most popular Vikram-ādityan legends, e.g., those told by thirtytwo images, the man in the street is familiar with the anecdote of the great romantic love between Kām Kāndhlā and Madho, which in its tragic intensity reminds one of Laila and Majnun. Such love-stories have not been *tabu* in Indian life and thought.

The Hindu knows how the God of Gods wants to be a cultivator and tiller of the soil. Shiva's consultation with his consort Pārvatī (lit. Mountain's Daughter), Pārvatī's lending a helping hand to everything he does, the little altercations between the two, and things like that constitute no small part of the poetry of actual life in India. One of the most touching is the story of Pārvatī's putting on a pair of conch-shell bracelets. These bracelets are the emblems of married life to be put on so long as the husband is alive. The story has thus a most sacred association with all married women. It acquires its specially romantic character from the fact that it is Shiva, the husband of Pārvatī, who has come in the disguise of a pedlar to sell these bracelets. Pārvatī meets him and Shiva is trying the bracelets on her hands but condemns her as being too stiff-muscled. There is a good deal of humour in this little action.

There is a "comedy of errors" also in Shaiva literature. The Hindu knows the story of Shiva's forgetting his own wife and taking liberties with some other lady whom he mistakes for Pārvatī. Further, the story of the awakening of Shiva's amorous passion through the instrumentality of Madana or Eros is too well known. This was necessary in the interest of Heaven's defence against the Titans. It had been ordained that the child of Shiva through Pārvatī could be the only victor over the foe. But Shiva had then been in meditation and vow of celibacy. Madana, the great awakener of sex-desire, was therefore called upon to play his part. He was successful—the result was the birth of Kumāra, magnificently told in Kālidāsa's *Kumāra Sambhava*.

It has to be noted that if we have the triumph of sex-passion here, we have also the burning or destruction of Madana, the god of love, in the next episode. It is well known, again, how the control of sex-passions forms the motif of a vast mass of the literature of India. *Moha-mudgara* or "The Cudgelling of Senses" is a classic in that line.

All the *rasas* or passions from the loathsome and terrific to the delightful and carnal have thus been represented in the sex-factor of Hindu culture. The coarseness and realism of the *lingam*, the sweetness and romance of Rādhā, the sublimity and austere chastity of Sītā, the military prowess of the War-Lord, Kumāra, the cataclysmal destructive force of Rudra, and the terror of Kālī, have all to be recognised while interpreting any branch of Hindu sex-literature. Sex as sex has been in Indian thought as comprehensive as humanism itself. Herein lies the Hindu conception of the dignity of sex,—the sacredness of sex as an organ of the human system, apart from its social, economic, moral or political values. And those values also have not been ignored in art or in life.

The Hindu has never believed in the atrophy of any sense or sense-organ. He has therefore idealized and deified every human passion and every phase of human beauty. Sex with all its functions has thus its own apotheosis in the Hindu system of life and thought; and *Kāma-shāstra* or erotics is one of the oldest Indian sciences. The joys and griefs of amorous life are, therefore, as sacred as the joys and griefs of life in other spheres. Vidyāpati as the poet of sex-desire and physical beauty does not require any apology. He is the apostle of traditional Hindu humanism. And this Indian message has been presented to the larger world not a moment too soon in Coomāraswāmy's *Bangīya Padābalī*.

(b) *Sex-movements and Sex-sciences.*

And here it is necessary to point out that Vidyāpati's message, or the Hindu conception of the dignity of sex, must not be taken as equivalent to one or other of the many formulas that have become current in recent years through the movement of Feminism or "Woman's Rights," which has followed Socialism as one of the by-products of "Industrial Revolution." By dignity of sex are not to be meant the theories about female genius, male women, womanish men, sexual equality, co-education, subjection of women, or superiority of the female brain. By dignity of sex is not to be understood the prominence attached to such problems as "free love," polygamy, chastity, celibacy, divorce, "love-children," bastardism, romantic marriages, the choosing of love through one's own eyes, or the selection of brides through great-grandmothers as matchmakers. The message of the Hindu artists is quite independent of all these questions, problems, fads, studies or scientific hypotheses. The dignity of sex is the right of sex as sex, of sex as a factor in human life, of sex as a natural organ. This has no reference either to the alleged usurpation of woman's rights by man during the past, or to the alleged attempt on woman's part to recover these rights by overthrowing the tyranny of man in the present. Vidyāpati's formula for the sanctity of sex may be given in any one of the following dicta of Whitman:

> "If anything is sacred the human body is sacred."
>
> "The man's body is sacred, and the woman's body is sacred,
> No matter who it is, it is sacred."

And, "Without shame the man I like knows and avows the deliciousness of his sex,
Without shame the woman I like knows and avows hers."

Serious investigations of scientific researchers in pedagogics, medical jurisprudence, criminology, history of marriage, abnormal psychology and other branches of comparative psychology, ethnography and comparative anthropology, insanity, adolescence, and physiology of love, as well as aesthetics and religious fetishism, have been bringing to light marvellous facts about sex and its influence on the growth, development and individuation of personality. The out-look on life and its mysteries is thus being deepened and widened; and the very foundations of human logic, ethics, spirituality and legislation are being laid anew. The dignity of sex, however, is not necessarily dependent on the conclusions of this new branch of socio-natural philosophy.

The Rousseaus of the "Rights of Woman" have declared that the sexes are equal. "What man has done woman can do" is their cry. They have unearthed facts of culture-history to prove the quality, quantity and variety of female contributions to world's progress. What is required for the present, according to them, is only an equalization of opportunities for the female sex to vindicate its capability in every walk of life. This equalization is to be effected by a thorough overhauling of the laws relating to property, marriage, labour, suffrage, and last but not least, education. The watch-word of extreme feminists is co-education, and this not solely in matters of discipline and organization, but also in the subjects of instruction and research. Equality of sexes in the regime of this sexual democracy would be a species of sexual "monism" so to speak—a complete unsexing of humanity. By dignity of sex one need not commit oneself to this *reductio ad absurdum*. Nor need one have anything to do with the theory of the opposite school, e.g., that of Schopenhauerian misogynists, which demonstrates that "there is not a single woman in the history of thought who can be truthfully compared with men of fifth or sixth rate genius."

It has been said that "a woman's demand for emancipation and her qualification for it are in direct proportion to the amount of maleness in her, ... that the real female element has neither the desire nor the capacity for emancipation." Dr. Otto Weininger proves that the great "emancipated" women famous in history were not women at all whether psychologically or physiologically. Sappho, Catherine II of Russia, Queen Christina of Sweden, George Sand, Madame de Staal, Clara Schumann, George Eliot, Madame Blavatsky and others were "partly bi-sexual and partly homo-sexual." The dignity of sex would not be impaired even if these and other facts of female physiology, psychology, logic and ethics so mercilessly revealed by the author in his epochmaking *Sex and Character* were substantiated by subsequent students.

The dignity of sex does not depend on the final solution of the question of the rival claims of monogamy and polygamy as social institutions. Nor is it bound up with the more recent controversy raised through women's demanding an "equal standard of morality" from men in retaliation of the age-long male demand for female chastity. The modern woman has raised the cry "Give us white (pure) men!" To this legitimate demand for purer morals, the rigid scientist has presented the conclusion of his investigations in most ghastly terms. It is said that a woman is by nature bound to be monogamous but that a man is by nature bound to be polygamous! Problems like these do not, however, affect the rights of sex as sex.

Hindu scientists, poets, and philosophers from Charaka, Manu and Bhāsha downwards have had their own answers to these questions and their own solutions. But their conception of the sanctity of sex-impulse is not necessarily a deduction from these. The dignity of sex is a natural corollary to the dignity of the animal in man, the sacredness of the beast in humanity. Man is at bottom a cognate and colleague of the ape and tiger;

the science of man or anthropology is fundamentally grounded in zoology.

Tennyson expressed the pious wish: "And let the ape and tiger die." That wish is never to be fulfilled. Woe unto humanity if that wish were ever to be fulfilled. The tiger-element has given rise to the "Kurukshetras" and "armageddons" of world's history. The wars of the Homeric and Vālmīkian epics, the Celtic sagas and the Teutonic Nibelungenlied, have repeated themselves epoch by epoch to demonstrate the progress of civilization through the manifestations of the tiger in man. War is a cosmic force—it is a sociological necessity. The "dignity of war" has been the verdict of universal history. It has yet to be frankly accepted as the first postulate of social philosophy. The "right" of war, the "sacredness" of war, the dignity of war, would, however, soon be current coin in human phraseology.

Likewise, the ape-element in man, his sexual impulse or sensuality, has a right to reverence which is no longer to be withheld by philosophers, statesmen, artists and educators. The dignity of sex is, infact, to be the principal plank in the platform of neo-positivism during the coming decades. And this inspite of the recent monkish conclusion of an Austrian philosopher that "woman, as woman, must disappear, and until that has come to pass there is no possibility of establishing the 'Kingdom of God on earth,' and the pessimistic reflections of the older Schopenhauer and Hartmann.

The Psychology of Truth and Good, as well as of Beauty and Love, is at present oscillating between the extreme biological and extreme non-biological, the empiric-associational and the noumenal-transcendental, the sensational and metaphysical, poles. Probably this dualism of human science arising from the dualism of human life is eternal and will never be finally solved. Prof. Krafft-Ebing has announced in his *Psychopathia Sexualis:* "Sexual feeling is really the root of all ethics, and no doubt of aestheticism and religion." While this extreme doctrine of every high sentiment as being nothing but sublimated sexuality is being opposed by the neo-Kantian school of "Pure Reason" and "Practical Reason," mortals must pay the positivists their due in the following words of Whitman:

> "I accept Reality and dare not question it,
> Materialism first and last imbuing.
> Hurrah for positive science! long live exact demonstration!
> Gentlemen, to you the first honour always!
> Your facts are useful, and yet they are not my dwelling,
> I but enter by them to an area of my dwelling."

Advocacy of the right of sex is thus only a deduction from the recognition of the rights of "sense-man." It is, however, not blind to the mysteries of "untold life," of life's immensities, of the "Everlasting Nays" i.e., the fundamental question of human "personality," the "ego," the self, the *ātman*. It only leaves those questions open. It is even prepared to appreciate the "prag, matic" efficacy of the postulating of the "spirit"-man-of faith in a Divine Order of the Universe, and of the conceptions of immortality, re-incarnation, etc. It would thus not be inconsistent to hold with Matthew Arnold:

> "Man hath all that Nature hath, but more,
> And in that *more* lie all his hopes of good."

(c) *Sexual and Spiritual.*

The dignity of sex is brought home to us from an altogether unexpected quarter also. I am referring to philology, especially the philology of abstract terms, metaphors, similes and analogies. Everybody is well aware how the experiences of purely spiritual and absolutely non-secular life have to be recorded in the language of the senses, the tongue of sexual life in the last analysis. It may or may not be true that sex-impulse is the basis and awakener of the highest mystical ecstasies. But it is a fact that expressions of the most super-sensuous life have been in terms of the senses. The language of Divine Love, spiritual union, self-surrender to God, "monistic" "self-realization," and so forth, has been the language of sex. And it is because of this that the art of pure humanism is liable to be misinterpreted as allegory of transcendental life, or geniune spiritual experiences as horrible carnalism.

Vivek-ānanda, one of the greatest idealists of modern India was lecturing in America on the "Religion of Love." His primary object was to condemn the human love as hollow and unreal. His message is: "There cannot be any love but in God: why then all these loves? These are mere mistakes." If any sentiment could be non-sensual, that it was. But the very title of his lecture is "Intense Longing is the first step." Without context the headline is calculated to attract the Romeos and Juliets from the Broadways of U.S. cities.

This almost unconscious treatment of highest non-sensual impulses in terms of the sensual owing to the short-comings of human language should be carefully distinguished from the conscious and artistic fusion of the sexual and the spiritual which we find in the love-literature produced at "boiling-point." The motif there is purely human and secular impulse, but the presentation is almost transcendental. Walter Pater notices this blending of the earthly and divine in Dante;

"In him the material and spiritual are fused and blent; if the spiritual attains the definite visibility of a crystal, what is material loses its earthiness and impurity. And here again by force of instinct Rossetti is one with him." It may be said that every love-poem produced under these conditions would be a blending of the sexual and spiritual. Kālidāsa, Vidyāpati and Tāgore are likewise one with Dante and Rossetti.

A few lines from Rossetti's *Blessed Damozel* would illustrate this fusion:

"The blessed damozel leaned out
From the gold bar of heaven;
Her eyes were deeper than the depth
Of waters stilled at even.

* * *

Her hair that lay along her back
Was yellow like ripe corn.
Her seemed she scarce had been a day
One of God's choristers;
The wonder was not yet quite gone
From that still look of hers.

* * *

It was the rampart of God's house
That she was standing on.

* * *

And still she bowed herself and stooped
Out of the circling charm;
Until her bosom must have made
The bar she leaned on warm.

* * *

"I wish that he were come to me,
For he will come," she said.
"Have I not prayed in Heaven?—on earth,
Lord, Lord, has he not prayed?
Are not two prayers a perfect strength?
And shall I feel afraid?

* * *

"We two will lie in the shădow of
That living mystic tree.

* * *

"But shall God lift
To endless unity
The soul whose likeness with thy soul
Was but its love for thee?

* * *

"There will I ask of Christ the Lord
Thus much for him and me:—
Only to live as once on earth
With love,—only to be,
As then a while, for ever now
Together, I and he."

* * *

And then she cast her arms along
The golden barriers,
And laid her face between her hands,
And wept. (I heard her tears)."

The machinery and technique here are theological and mediaeval, the images called up and sentiments expressed are, however, thoroughly human. Here is a picture of intense love between man and woman,—an idea of the deepest grief—exhibited in bold relief against a sedate and almost ascetic treatment of Roman Catholic imageries. The sensuous and the spiritual have mingled—but the sensuous is not eclipsed. As Stopford Brooke remarks: "No one who has loved and lost, and waits here below or there above, but must have cherished its main thought and felt its main emotion."

The depth of sensuous longing and ecstasy is more felt than described in some of the love-songs of Tāgore's *Gardener*. Here is an instance:

"When I go alone at night to my love-tryst, birds do not sing, the wind does not stir, the houses on both sides of the street stand silent.

It is my own anklets that grow loud at every step and I am ashamed.

When I sit on my balcony and listen for his footsteps, leaves do not rustle on the trees, and the water is still in the river like the sound on the knees of a sentry fallen asleep.

It is my own heart that beats wildly—I do not know how to quiet it.

When my love comes and sits by my side, when my body trembles and my eyelids droop, the night darkens, the wind blows out the lamp, and the clouds draw veils over the stars.

It is the jewel at my own breast that shines and gives light. I do not know how to hide it."

In these lines we see the birds and trees, the

sentinel and the lamp and seem almost to forget the person of the love-impassioned speaker. And yet in her heart is the commotion of boiling emotion. This is the sensuous spiritualized—an excellent example of *samyama* or self-restraint in art. Tāgore has given us a picture of "those times in love between man and woman when, "to quote Stopford Brooke again, "the sensuous element is lifted by pure joy and emotion into the spiritual world and there transfigured; and when the spiritual element is brought into the sensuous till it is made, as it were, palpable, embodied, incarnated when both sense and spirit are fused into one fire."

This expression of the sensuous through the "fusion of sense and spirit" is to be distinguished from the expression of the super-sensuous or spiritual in and through the sensuous. Let us hear Vivek-ānanda lecturing on *Bhakti* or Devotion (spiritual love):

"Love knows no fear. How can you frighten love? Does the lamb love the lion? The mouse the cat? The slave the master? Slaves sometimes simulate love, but is it love? Where do you ever see love in fear? It is always sham. ......Think of a young mother in the street and a dog barking at her; she flies into the next house. Suppose the next day she is in the street with her child and a lion is upon the child; where will be her position? Just in the mouth of the lion, protecting her child. Love conquers all fear. So also is love to God. Who cares whether God is a rewarder or a punisher? That is not the thought of a lover. Think of a judge when he comes home, what does his wife see in him? Not a judge or a rewarder, or a punisher, but her husband, her lover.

How many times we see one of the handsomest of men love a very ugly woman. Where is the attraction to them? Those that are standing aside see the ugly man, or the ugly woman, but not the lover. To the lover they are the most beautiful beings that ever existed. How is it? The woman who was loving the ugly man took, as it were, the ideal of beauty which was in her own brain, and projected it over this ugly man.

What is it that makes atoms come and join atoms, molecule, molecule, sets big planets flying towards each other, attracts man to woman, woman to man, human beings to human beings, animals to animals, drawing the whole universe, as it were, towards one centre? This is called love. ......What is manifesting itself as attraction in the sentient and the insentient, in the particular and the universal, is the love of God. ......

Thus sang the royal Hebrew sage, thus sang they of India. "O beloved, one kiss of Thy lips! One that has been kissed by Thee, his thrist for Thee increaseth for ever. All sorrows cease, and he forgets the past, present and future, and only thinks of Thee alone." That is the madness of the lover, when all desires have vanished. Who cares for salvation? Who cares to be saved? Who cares to be perfect even? Who cares for freedom? So says the lover.

I do not want wealth, no, not even health. I do not want beauty, do not want intellect; let me be born again, and again, amid all the evils that are in the world; I will not complain, but let me love Thee, and that for love's sake."

The prophet of neo-Vedāntism, the apostle of superhuman, other-worldly and transcendental truths, the "scorner of the ground," has thus to express himself throughout and deliver his entire message only in terms of the human, the worldly, the "sense"-man. He wants us to draw upon our sensuous experiences, the "dirt," the "dust," the flesh, the animal in man inorder to understand the truths of the "only real" life and love. This lecture on spiritual love has the following towards the close: "Most attractive human love is that between the sexes and it was therefore that language which they took up. It was the madness of sexual love that was the faintest echo of the mad love of the saint." This, then, is the dignity of the sensuous, the sacredness of the sex, that the highest life has to be interpreted in terms of the sensuous and the sexual. Truly, "herein lies an imperfection which yet is noble and grand."

Coomāraswāmy quotes for us the following from a mediaeval Christian hymn "in which the language of human love is deliberately adapted to religious uses:"

> "When ye se blosmes springe,
> And here foules songe,
> A suete love-longynge
> Myn herte thourh out stong;
> Al for a love newe,
> That is so suete and trewe,
> That gladieth al mi song.

Here the "new love" is Christ."

Coomāraswāmy quotes the following from Hafiz (translated by Walter Leaf):

> "Cowl of the monk and bowl of wine, how shall the twain by man be wed?

Yet for the love I bear to thee, these to unite I dare for thee."

Such passages may be quoted also from Jami, Rumi, Sādi, Abul Ala and other Persian mystics.

The Jōdō Buddhist of Japan, also, like the Vedāntist, the Christian and the Sufi, realizes spiritual love through the medium of the sensuous or secular. We get the following account of Jōdōism or Japanese *Bhakti*-cult in Okakura's *Ideals of the East*: "A wave of religious emotion passed over Japan in the Fujiwara epoch (A.D. 900–1200), and intoxicated with frantic love, men and women deserted the cities and villages in crowds to follow Kuya or Ipen, dancing and singing the name of Āmidā as they went. Masquerades came into vogue, representing angels descending from heaven with lotus dais, inorder to welcome and bear upward the departing soul. Ladies would spend a life time in weaving or embroidering the image of Divine Mercy, out of threads extracted from the lotus stem. Such was the new movement, which......closely paralleled in China in the beginning of the Tāng dynasty (618–905)......has never died, and to this day two thirds of the people belong to the Jōdō sect, which corresponds to the Vaishnavism of India. Both Genshin, the formulator of the creed, and Genku, who carried it to its culmination, pleaded that human nature was weak, and try as it might, could not accomplish entire self-conquest and direct attainment of the Divine in this life." The Jōdō and Vaishnava expressions of spiritual life and thought are thus preeminently human.

We have seen Vivek-ānandā's use of the sensuous to describe the super-sensuous. Kabīr, the fifteenth century mystic of Hindusthan, also, had to do the same. Says Underhill in Tāgore's *Kabīr*: "It is by the simplest metaphors, by constant appeals to needs, passions which all men understand—the bridegroom and bride, the guru and disciple, the pilgrim, the farmer, the migrant bird—that he drives home his intense conviction of the reality of the soul's intercourse with the Transcendent. .... This willing acceptance of the here-and-now as a means of representing supernal realities is a trait common to the greatest mystics. Their fearless employment of homely and physical symbols—often startling and even revolting to the unaccustomed taste—is in direct proportion to the exaltation of their spiritual life. The works of the great Sufis, and amongst the Christians, of Jacopone da Todi, Ruysbroeck, Boehme, abound in illustrations of this law."

Kabīr sings:

"When I am parted from my Beloved, my heart is full of misery: I have no comfort in the day, I have no sleep in the night. To whom shall I tell my sorrow?

The night is dark; the hours slip by. Because my Lord is absent, I start up and tremble with fear.

Kabīr says: "Listen, my friend! there is no other satisfaction save in the encounter with the Beloved."

All this smacks of "the heart of a woman."

Sensuous love, when most glowing, utters itself in terms of spiritual or religious or mystical ecstasy. To men and women under the influence of this passion there is nothing higher than love, love is their "highest good," the only reality. "Love is and was their Lord and King." The world of lovers is an "earthly paradise," and they are tempted to describe their experience in terms of paradise, angels, and so forth, simply because it is customary to associate anything great with the unknown world of spirit. But the weakness of the spiritual world is too patent when one is required to define the ecstasy of life in that region. All "God-intoxicated men," people who have drunk deep of the celestial bliss, the mystics and seers of the transcendental truths have to declare their Divine Union and Infinite Love in terms of the sexual union, the raptures of sensuous love. They do not seem to know of anything higher than this! The sacredness of sex does not require any further evidence. And this is independent of the validity or otherwise of the alleged identity of all forms of love, i.e., apart from the value to be attached to the extremist mystical equation, Sexual Ecstasy = Spiritual Ecstasy.

The love of Rādhā and Krishna is human love, generally speaking. But it became the conventional symbol also of Love Divine, the attraction between the Soul and God in mediaeval Indian thought, the "plasm" of Bhakti cult. Rādhā may then be said to have stood for the Beatrice of Hindu Dantes, who began to "write concerning her what hath not before been written of any woman." Chinese literary tradition also knows of such "types" of romantic and mystic love between man and woman, e.g., those immortalized by the great Po Chu-i in his *Everlasting Wrong*, of which the hero is the Tāng Emperor Ming Huang. But to see one grand allegory of spiritual experience in the whole mass of Rādhā-Krishna lyrics is more than can be accepted. Vidyāpati, at any rate, in his Idylls of Rādhā, is not at all swayed by the allegoristic tendency. He is a humanist *par excellence*, the poet of human desires, sensuous passions, and physical beauty. If his songs have been partly or wholly taken as symbolical of the super-human, it is because of the names, Rādhā and Krishna, which, in popular imagination, have always had a religious association. But "higher criticism" must disentangle humanism from mediaeval symbolism forced upon it by the despotism of tradition. The Beatrice of Dante's *New Life* is different from the Beatrice of his *Divine Comedy*. So there are Rādhās and Rādhās in mediaeval Vaishnava lore.

(d) *The Futurism of Young India.*

Vikramorvasie, *Padābali* and *Chitrā* are all studies in humanism. Their theme is sensuous love, the dignity of sex. This Hindu conception is a distinct contribution to the world culture of the present day. It has been brought to the forefront at a time when the dignity of sex has been attracting universal attention. For whatever be the value of the sex-movements and the sex-sciences of the last two decades or so, interest in sex as sex has come to stay. During the last century the "dignity of work," i.e., the "sanctity of labour," has been planted as an axiom in human consciousness through the efforts of Carlyle and Morris, Karl Marx and Ferdinand Lassale, Louis Blanc and Mazzini, Whitman and Emerson, Dayānanda and Vivek-ānanda. Similarly the dignity of sex is going to be established as one of the A.B.C.'s of modern thought by the middle of the twentieth century.

The humanism revived by Aurobinda Ghosh, Coomāraswāmy and Tāgore has a special significance for Hindu culture also. Hindu classicism and Indian mediaevalism are feeding the omnivorous Romanticism of Young India. This romanticism does not exhaust itself, however, in antiquarian and archaeological revivals, and in brooding over the dead past, but is a vitalizing force and constructs from far and near new ideals of life and art to inspire the present. And these ideals forged in the laboratory of Young India's brain are keeping pace with the world-forces of the modern age. Young India is thus not an isolated or exceptional phenomenon but an integral part of the world-system—an eddy among the eddies of a vast whirlpool.

The deeper meaning of *The Hero and the Nymph*, "The Idylls of Rādhā," and *Chitra* to Young India is that Hindu culture has been brought in line with the present-day tendencies in literature and art. Hindu culture has ever been a living, moving, growing and expanding culture. Young India, therefore, does not look back to the Indo-Moslem Renaissance of the sixteenth and seventeenth centuries under the Great Moghuls, or to the Vikram-ādityan greatness of Hindu culture from the fourth to the twelfth century, or the still earlier epoch of Maurya glory (third century B.C.), as an adequately inspiring ideal. The heart of Young India is burning with the aspirations and emotions of modern mankind, its brain is teeming with suggestions and ideas for supplying the world's pressing needs.

Young India does not think of culture in terms of geographical or political boundaries, but solely as a body of universal truths and achievements for the furtherance of humanity's progress. Young India believes that *Kultur* can never be "national" except only in politics, but that it is always human and cosmopolitan. It is the problem of the world from the Indian angle that Young India seeks to solve. Young India aims to contribute its own discoveries in science, industry, philosophy and social service to the widening stream of human civilization and thus to be recognized as a force among the forces of the universe. It is the ambition of Young India to be nothing short of a first-class power on the platform of modern world culture.

Young India is thus modernist or rather "futurist." The culture of modern Hindusthan is neither a mere restoration nor a *re*presentation of the mediaeval and ancient life and achievements. It is utilising and assimilating the world-energies of today and also creating fresh forces and sending them abroad for mankind. Young India is looking forward to a nobler and happier future of the human race and intends to make Hindu culture an instrument of that future. This futurism is the life-blood of Young India's idealists and dreamers.

The futurism of Young India can be expressed in the enthusiastic hope of Shelley:

> "Another Athens shall arise,
> And to remoter time
> Bequeath, like sunset to the skies,
> The splendour of its prime;
> And leave, if naught so bright may live,
> All earth can take or Heaven can give.
> The world is weary of the past,
> Oh, might it die or rest at last!"

Young India does not live in memory of the past

but has inspiring visions for the future. Satyendranāth Datta has sung in Bengali for whole India:

> "Futureward we cast gleeful longing glance."

Kumudnāth Lāhirī's call, also, is the message of futurism:

> "Why to manhood this insult,—why?
> Mind not the present source of grief;
> The fetters of swoon to pieces shatter
> Bold with eyes on future far."

The "criticism of life," finally, in the humanist art presented by Tāgore, Coomāraswāmy, and Aurobinda Ghosh, is—

Futureward Ho!